W9-CNG-668

Weekend
Kitchen
Makeovers

Weekend
Kitchen
Makeovers

Paul Ryan

with Bridget Biscotti Bradley

LARK
BOOKS

A Division of Sterling Publishing Co., Inc.
New York

10 9 8 7 6 5 4 3 2 1

First Edition

Published by Lark Books, A Division of
Sterling Publishing Co., Inc.
387 Park Avenue South, New York, N.Y. 10016

Text © 2006, Lark Books
Photography © 2006, DIY Network
Illustrations © 2006, Lark Books

Distributed in Canada by Sterling Publishing,
c/o Canadian Manda Group, 165 Dufferin Street
Toronto, Ontario, Canada M6K 3H6

Distributed in the United Kingdom by GMC Distribution Services,
Castle Place, 166 High Street, Lewes, East Sussex, England BN7 1XU

Distributed in Australia by Capricorn Link (Australia) Pty Ltd.,
P.O. Box 704, Windsor, NSW 2756 Australia

The written instructions, photographs, designs, patterns, and projects in this volume are intended for
the personal use of the reader and may be reproduced for that purpose only. Any other use, especially
commercial use, is forbidden under law without written permission of the copyright holder.

Every effort has been made to ensure that all the information in this book is accurate. However, due
to differing conditions, tools, and individual skills, the publisher cannot be responsible for any injuries,
losses, and other damages that may result from the use of the information in this book.

If you have questions or comments about this book, please contact:
Lark Books
67 Broadway
Asheville, NC 28801
(828) 253-0467

Manufactured in China

All rights reserved

ISBN 13: 978-1-57990-918-5
ISBN 10: 1-57990-918-3

For information about custom editions,
special sales, premium and corporate purchases,
please contact Sterling Special Sales Department
at 800-805-5489 or specialsales@sterlingpub.com.

Series Editor: Dawn Cusick
Managing Editor: Bridget Biscotti Bradley
Series Designer: Thom Gaines
Page Design and Production: Maureen Spuhler
Cover Designer: DIY Network
Illustrator: Ian Worpole
Production Assistant: Matt Paden
Copy Editor: John Edmonds

Contents

Weekend
Kitchen Makeovers

I love it when people come up to me and say, "Let me ask you a question about my kitchen." It usually means they are thinking of a change, and that gets my wheels turning. I truly enjoy working with people to solve their kitchen problems, whether the issues are related to design or function.

When I was growing up and we had visitors, my mom and dad used to disappear behind the kitchen door to prepare the food. We could hear them working and the delicious smells would waft into the dining room, but more often than not we weren't allowed in the kitchen to watch or even help them. "It's too crowded in here," my mom always said. In today's households, just the opposite is true. The kitchen has become a gathering place for families and their friends, and homeowners want larger, more open spaces in which to work and entertain.

Families change over time, and many people want their kitchens to change along with them. If you expect your family to grow, you may need a larger or safer space. If your children are moving out, maybe that center island that was once a hub of activity now just seems to be in the way.

Style and technology change, too. If every time you look at your run-down cabinets or that stained countertop you think you can do

better, you probably can. If you turn on that old vent hood and the motor grinds loudly but does little to remove steam and odors, or if you don't run your dishwasher at night because the noise keeps you awake, it may be time to think about a change.

Whatever your reason, I encourage you to take the plunge and create a kitchen that fits your current needs. Planning a large project like a kitchen remodel can take time, so don't rush the process. Keep in mind that you are the one who has to live with the finished space. Do your research, find the materials and appliances that will fit your needs, and interview several contractors for any parts of the job you might not be able to do yourself. Then come up with a schedule. While surprises can and do happen, it helps to be somewhat prepared for how long you'll be without a working kitchen. I know it seems daunting now, but before long you'll have the kitchen of your dreams and the pride of being able to point to some or all of it and say, "I did that!"

So what are you waiting for?

Paul

Paul Ryan,
Host of DIY Network's *Kitchen Renovations*

Weekend Kitchen Makeovers

1

Planning Your Kitchen Renovation

Try to have an open mind when you take on a project as significant as a kitchen remodel. The advice I give people is to lower their expectations. What I mean by that is you should expect the worst, and when good things happen, you will be pleasantly surprised.

If you start this project thinking everything will go smoothly and you get crossed up along the way, you will get frustrated more easily. When I'm removing appliances in a project, I expect the electrical to be hard to remove. When I'm taking out a sink, I expect that the shutoffs will be rusted or missing. When I experience the opposite, like when the shutoffs do work, the job seems easier.

If you keep this in mind throughout the project, you will experience less frustration and more satisfaction. This advice is not meant to make you lower your expectations for the final look and function of the kitchen. I just want you to keep in mind that nothing is as easy as it seems. When we do our TV shows, we spend a lot of time when the camera is not rolling making sure everything is going according to plan. I know it may sound hard to believe, but we have surprises all the time on location and we have to roll with the punches to make it work.

If you get frustrated along the way, just step back and consider the final result. It's a lot of work now, but when it's done, you will have a space that you can enjoy for years to come.

Paul

Except for adding on to your home, remodeling your kitchen is the biggest, most expensive, most disruptive home improvement project you can undertake. Most people realize this and end up living with an outdated or dysfunctional kitchen for years because the idea of going through a kitchen remodel is so overwhelming. But it doesn't have to be. By taking your time to plan out every detail in advance, hiring the right people to help you with what you can't do yourself, and sticking to your decisions, you can make the process relatively painless. Once you've finished, you'll be so happy with your new kitchen that you may wonder why you didn't do this years ago.

The money you are about to spend is significant, but in most housing markets you will get a high rate of return on your investment as long as you go with a style that works with the rest of your house. If you plan on living in your home for the foreseeable future, then you'll want to make your kitchen look and function in a way that works best for you and your family. But if you plan to sell your home within the next five years, it pays to choose a more traditional design, allow for standard-size appliances, and build in as much storage space as possible. If you can't spend the money to do it right, some real estate professionals would advise that you not completely remodel your kitchen but instead do a minor face-lift to make it look its best for the time being. This book will show you how to do it all, from quick makeovers to full renovations.

SCOPE OF THE PROJECT

It's usually fairly obvious when a kitchen isn't working. Are your cabinets shoddily constructed or falling apart? Do you not have enough storage space, or are the cabinets not configured so you have the right utensils or appliances where you need them? If this is the case, you probably need to replace or reconfigure the cabinets. On the other hand, if they are in good shape and meet your needs but you don't like the way they look, you can paint them or have them professionally refaced.

Replacing the cabinets constitutes a significant remodel. Your existing cabinets and countertop will be torn out, so it's the perfect time to reconfigure the room, update plumbing and wiring as needed, and plan a new lighting scheme. You can choose to keep the existing flooring and appliances, or opt for a new floor and built-in appliances. This is also an opportunity to alter the workflow of the room and change the location of the sink, refrigerator, or range. Doing this will cost more money, as plumbing, gas, and electrical lines will need to be extended, but it's well worth the extra expense to get things where you want them while you have the opportunity to do so.

You may even decide to expand the kitchen into an adjoining room or closet by removing some walls. Other options are small bump-outs or whole room additions. These are much larger endeavors, as you'll need to extend your home's foundation and roofline. Hire an architect, if you plan to go this route, to make sure your addition blends seamlessly with the existing structure.

If you like the current configuration of your kitchen and the cabinets are either working as they are or are good candidates to be refaced, then consider a simple makeover. Replacing the floors or countertop, adding a colorful backsplash, replacing an old appliance, and installing new light fixtures can make a huge difference in the way your kitchen looks and functions for a fraction of the cost of a full remodel.

Whichever option you choose, be sure to plan out the project from start to finish and get the right building permits before you reach for your tool bag. Renovating any room requires a detailed plan because the work has to be accomplished in a certain order. Write up a list of all the things you want to do, such as removing the existing floor, installing new countertops, or painting the walls. Next to each task, write down whether you have the materials you need now, can get the materials quickly, or need to order in advance (many elements of a kitchen remodel need significant lead times). Then make a final list of the order of work, taking labor and materials needs into consideration.

After demolition and any structural modifications are completed, a typical order of work is new flooring, plumbing and electrical changes, drywall, cabinet installation, wall texture and painting, countertops, appliance hook-ups, fixtures, and finishing touches.

Sometimes the only way to really get what you want is with a complete remodel, which is what the owners of this kitchen did. In the end, they got a brighter and more spacious kitchen with the materials and colors they love.

CAN YOU DO THE WORK YOURSELF?

Doing the work yourself will give you an amazing sense of pride and accomplishment when the job is done. There's nothing like standing back and admiring the results of a room you've renovated on your own. But at the beginning of a project, the scope of the work may seem daunting. Many people think they need to commit to doing all of the construction work themselves, or none of it. However, you can choose to do some of the work yourself, like demolition, tiling, and painting, and leave less desirable or more complicated jobs to a professional.

Think about how much time you have to devote to this project. Unlike with other rooms in the house, you have only one kitchen. While it's under construction, you will have to find other ways to feed your

Installing a resilient floor is an example of a do-it-yourself project that doesn't require any special skills or tools.

TIPS | DIY Network Home Improvement

BUILDING CODES AND PERMITS

Before you start a kitchen renovation, take your plans to the local building authority and apply for the permits you need. The building authority will be able to tell you how many permits are required, whether you have to hire a professional for any portions of the job, and at what stages the work must be inspected. It is ultimately your responsibility to arrange for any required inspections. If the work doesn't meet code or hasn't been inspected, it may need to be ripped out and done over. Renovating your kitchen without the required permits is illegal and may even invalidate your homeowner's insurance.

family, wash dishes, and perhaps do the laundry, if the washer and dryer are also in the kitchen. Some families set up a temporary kitchen in another room of the house or in the garage. Consider this option if you have a place with a working sink and the electrical supply to run a few appliances. For major remodels that will take months, it pays to hire plumbers and electricians to set up a temporary kitchen for you. If you will be displaced for only a few weeks, you can probably get by with paper plates, a refrigerator, and a microwave.

It can save you a considerable amount of money to tackle a job yourself. About 25 percent of the cost of a remodel can be attributed to labor —more if you're moving fixtures or structurally changing the room. Those savings can be diminished, however, if you don't already own the tools you'll need. Professionals factor the cost of tools into their bids. Rented tools can save you money but will require time to track down, pick up, clean, and return. You'll also need to be organized and follow a schedule so that you're not paying a day rate on a tool that you're not ready to use. Also consider how much your time is worth. An experienced professional with the right tools can likely complete a job in a fraction of the time that you can. But if you enjoy the process and you or your family can handle the inconvenience, then you may be able to do most of the work yourself.

Cosmetic improvements such as installing a new tile backsplash, painting, and tiling a floor that's in good shape can be accomplished by anyone who has the time and interest to tackle them. If you're adding a large, heavy item like a professional-grade range or refrigerator, you'll need to make sure that your floor is sturdy enough to hold the weight and that your plumbing and electrical systems can support the added demand. If you're not sure, it's best to hire a professional for those aspects of the job.

ABOVE: Removing your own fixtures, appliances, and cabinets can save thousands of dollars. LEFT: Professionals have the tools that make a job easier and faster, such as this cabinet lift, which helps raise upper cabinets into place. Homeowners can often rent tools like these.

If you are leaving major fixtures like the sink, range, and refrigerator in the same spots, and if everything is in good working order with no leaks or corrosion, then the remodel will be much more manageable. Whenever you get into rerouting water supply and drain lines or undertaking major electrical upgrades, a project gets more complicated. It's better to hire a professional for those parts of the job rather than create future problems with shoddy work if you're not sure how to do them and can't take the time to learn. Also keep in mind that a general contractor will handle getting the building permits and scheduling inspections; otherwise, you will need to work with the local building department yourself.

WANTS VERSUS NEEDS

To help determine whether you can keep your existing floor plan or need to change it, make a list of wants versus needs. Open all those cupboards and drawers and take inventory of what you have in your kitchen now. Chances are there are small appliances, cooking supplies, and dishes that you don't use and have no intention of using. Take them out and donate them to a local charitable organization. Figure out how many cabinets and drawers you need to hold what remains, with a little room for growth. If you have appliances or fixtures that don't work properly, replacing them would fall under the needs category. A pro-style range may fall under wants, to be considered only if you can afford one after accounting for everything else.

ABOVE: Adding a spigot behind the range allows you to fill pots without having to lug them from the sink. This feature is a necessity for some people and a nicety for others. LEFT: Caffeine lovers may choose to make space for a home espresso counter.

Think about the way the current space functions and what it would take to make it work better. Is it common for two or more cooks to be working in the kitchen? If everyone wants to use the sink at the same time, consider adding a prep sink in another part of the kitchen or on an island. Does the dishwasher open right in front of the door to the kitchen, preventing people from coming and going while the dishes are being loaded? Moving the dishwasher to another spot would be a valuable change.

Take storage needs into account. If you have other places to store extra cleaning supplies and paper products, then you might not need as much storage space in the kitchen. If you need more storage, consider installing a tall cabinet at one end of the kitchen to store non-food-related items, extra shelves to hold cookbooks, and a place for recyclables.

What other needs could a kitchen remodel meet in your house? Are you lacking a space to pay bills or an area that the kids can use for homework? Do you need a laundry area? Is the dining room inconvenient for quick meals and you'd like to have a place to eat at the counter? This is the time to think big.

The owners of this kitchen can now sip their morning coffee while sitting at the counter. A flat-screen television keeps them up to date with the morning news while they make breakfast.

SAFETY

Follow these guidelines and protect yourself at all times.

◢ Always shut off the power before working on an electrical outlet. Then use a circuit tester to double-check that there is no power coming to the wires before you begin working on it.

◢ Always wear eye protection when using a power tool.

◢ Wear earplugs when using loud power tools.

◢ Never disturb an area that may contain asbestos. If the area must be disturbed, hire a profes-sional asbestos removal company to deal with it safely.

◢ Protect your back while lifting heavy objects. Use your legs and never twist your back while lifting.

◢ Wear heavy rubber gloves to protect your skin from chemicals.

◢ Test any paint that may have been applied prior to 1980 for lead before removing it. You can purchase lead test kits from home improvement centers. If you determine there is lead in the paint, seal off the room with plastic sheeting, and wear a respirator, goggles, gloves, and protective clothing when removing it. Then clean the area with a particulate vacuum cleaner designed to remove lead paint. Leave no dust behind. If you have a large amount of lead paint to sand or remove, call a professional.

◢ Wear dust masks when sanding wood surfaces or joint compound. It's often easier to breathe with a respirator than a dust mask, and respirators do a better job of protecting your lungs from fine dust particles.

WHEN TO HIRE HELP

Because kitchen remodels are often large and complicated and most people want them to be finished as quickly as possible, it's most common to hire out some or all of the work. Do-it-yourselfers may choose to take on some of the construction and/or act as the general contractor by hiring specialists for jobs they don't have the skills or time to do. Others may hire a general contractor to manage most of the construction, then complete the finish work themselves. Consider hiring the following professionals for certain situations.

Stone slab countertops must be installed by professionals. You can find and hire someone for the job, or your general contractor can call on one of his or her favorite subcontractors.

KITCHEN DESIGNERS

Even if you plan to do most of the work yourself, the services of a kitchen designer may be invaluable. The home improvement center or local shop you purchase cabinets from may offer free design services when you place an order, or charge you a certain amount of money up front that may go toward your purchase. You can also hire an independent kitchen designer who will tell you about all the latest appliances and fixtures available and advise you on everything from the layout to materials choices. The designer then creates schematic drawings, which you will need to order countertops and other materials, and to get bids from contractors. You can also use these drawings when you apply for a building permit. Designers understand plumbing and electrical requirements, construction methods, and local building codes. Their expertise can save you a lot of research, and they may even save you some money by identifying possible problems up front.

Certified kitchen designers have years of experience in planning and executing residential kitchen remodels. As with any accreditation process, they must pass tests and participate in ongoing education. Look for a designer who lists CKD (certified kitchen designer) next to his or her name.

There are many webites that can help you find a qualified professional in your area. Make appointments with several designers. Ask to see examples of their recent work and spend a little time with them in your current kitchen to determine whether you like their ideas and can communicate with them easily. Call a few of their recent clients and then select a designer that you feel comfortable with. Designers charge either an hourly rate or a flat fee that is a percentage of the overall project cost.

ARCHITECTS

If your kitchen remodel involves adding on a room to the house, bumping out an exterior wall, removing or altering existing interior walls, reconfiguring the space to turn it into a great room, or

Working with an architect is well worth the expense; they can ease many of the burdens associated with a large-scale remodel.

adding several new windows or skylights, the services of an architect are well worth the expense. Architects will make sure that your plans harmonize with the existing proportions of the house. They can advise you on everything from structural changes to project management and give you the drawings you'll need to obtain a building permit.

GENERAL CONTRACTORS

There are many parts to a kitchen remodel, and usually you will need at least one or two subcontractors to do things that you may not be able to do yourself. A general contractor will manage the project, deal with the local building department and permit process, and hire and supervise subcontractors. While you can perform this role yourself, it does take a lot of time and organization. It's also possible that a homeowner offering just one job might have a difficult time getting good subcontractors to show up. Even if you want to do some of the con-

struction work yourself, you can still have a general contractor supervise the project. Ask whether the contractor will stay on the job site every day until the work is done. Some who are juggling multiple projects at once have been known to leave a job for days or weeks at a time, which is the last thing you want when your kitchen is torn up.

Get bids from a few different contractors and give each of them the same detailed specifications for what you want done. If you put the project out to bid before knowing the scope of the remodel and the kinds of materials and appliances you want, contractors will likely bid high to cover higher-end materials. So know what you want before you call. Be prepared to pay some money up front to cover start-up costs, but that amount should never be more than 30 percent of the total job cost. A written schedule of payments that are linked to progress made should be part of the contract.

ASSESSING THE SPACE

It's useful to make a rough drawing of your kitchen, even if you plan to hire a professional designer or architect. Whomever you get to help you with this project will want to know the basic specifications of the room and how you want to change it.

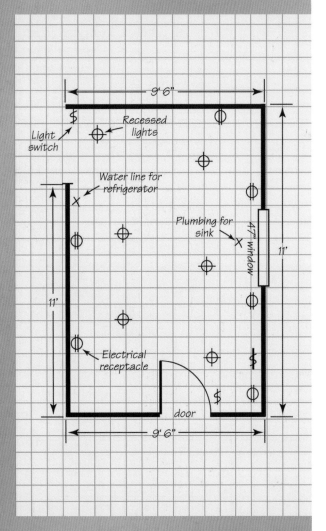

Use graph paper to make a base plan of your existing kitchen. Draw the room to scale, noting the size and location of windows and doors, and locations of electrical receptacles and lighting fixtures. Once you have this basic drawing, make several copies and use them to try out various configurations of your new kitchen. Include all the appliances, and try to decide where each cabinet element (such as deep or shallow drawers, corner pieces, upper and lower cabinets) should go. You may want to draw elevations of each wall to get a better sense of how the pieces will look next to one another, or transfer your information to a computer program that can show you the room from all angles.

VENTILATION

If you hire a professional designer, this may be as far as you need to go in drawing up the plan. Otherwise, consider whether you are leaving enough space between each major area. These industry-standard measurements will help:

- The standard height for countertops is 36 inches; depth of base cabinet is 24 inches.

- Eating counters are 36 to 42 inches high.

- There should be at least 42 inches between an island and the countertop, sink, refrigerator, or range.

- There should be at least 36 inches between an island and the traffic corridor.

- Leave at least 20 inches in front of an open dishwasher.

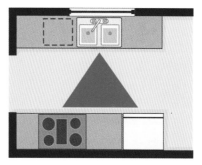

galley

◢◣ KITCHEN DESIGN ◢◣

Kitchen designers often utilize the work triangle, a term that refers to the placement of the refrigerator, sink, and range, and their relationship to one another. The three legs of the triangle should be no shorter than 4 feet and no longer than 9 feet, meaning that each of the three major elements (refrigerator, sink, and range) should be no less than 4 and no more than 9 feet apart. Very large kitchens with more than one refrigerator or sink may have overlapping work triangles. Most kitchens fall into one of these categories:

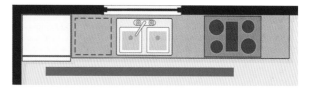

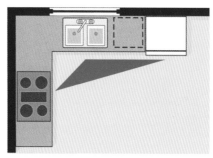

one-wall

◢◣ **GALLEY KITCHENS** have an entry-exit on each end with cabinets and countertops lining parallel walls.

◢◣ **ONE-WALL KITCHENS** have the sink, refrigerator, and range all on the same wall.

◢◣ **L-SHAPED KITCHENS** have work areas on adjacent walls and can include an island.

◢◣ **U-SHAPED KITCHENS** have work areas on three adjacent walls.

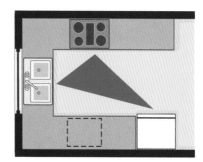

L-shaped

◢◣ **G-SHAPED KITCHENS** are basically U-shaped kitchens with an extra stretch of cabinets at one end.

Before deciding on a layout, consider the common traffic patterns in your kitchen. It's best to place the refrigerator at the outer corner of the cooking area so that people can walk in to get a snack without getting in your way when you're attending to hot pans on the stove. Also think about how traffic from adjacent areas, such as the dining room or family room, will affect your plan. Don't place the dishwasher in a spot where it will open into the doorway that people walk through with stacks of dishes from the kitchen table, for example.

U-shaped

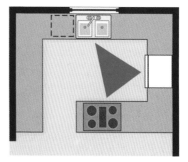

G-shaped

UNIVERSAL DESIGN

The principles of universal design aren't just for people with disabilities. They simply make the kitchen easier to use for all people, whether they are very tall, confined to a wheelchair, or have limited hand strength. Therefore, it makes sense to build a new kitchen with universal design principles in mind so it can be used comfortably by everyone, now and in the future.

Consider raising the dishwasher so that you don't have to bend down as far to load and unload it (you'll appreciate it when you're older). Replace the range with a separate cooktop and wall oven so that the oven can be placed at shoulder height. There should be enough space next to each appliance for you to set dishes or hot pans without carrying them across the room right after they are removed from the cooktop, microwave, or dishwasher. Very tall or very short people should plan for one or more sections of the countertop to be raised or lowered so they have a comfortable spot to prepare meals. People with limited hand strength will have an easier time using lever handles to open cabinets, and a single-lever faucet rather than one with separate hot and cold handles. Everyone can benefit from slip-resistant flooring, rounded edges on countertops, balanced lighting plans, and anti-scald valves on faucets to prevent burns.

Single-handle faucets can be operated with one hand, and rounded countertop edges prevent injuries.

This cooktop and sink were placed over open areas so that someone in a wheelchair, or someone who needs to sit while working in the kitchen, can use them with ease.

SPECIAL-NEEDS OPTIONS

For people who are confined to a wheelchair, consider the following guidelines for kitchen design:

◢ All openings and doorways should be at least 34 inches wide.

◢ Traffic aisles should be at least 36 inches wide.

◢ There should be a turnaround area of at least 30 by 48 inches in front of every appliance.

◢ The sink should be 32 inches high and no more than 6 inches deep.

◢ Under the sink, there should be a 27-inch-high, 19-inch-deep clearance for wheelchairs, and any exposed pipes should be insulated to prevent leg burns.

◢ The handles for daily-use storage areas, plus light switches and electrical receptacles, should be no higher than 48 inches from the floor.

diy
network

BUDGET

The most economical way to upgrade a kitchen is to keep most of what you have and give one or more surfaces (like the cabinets or countertops) a face lift. If you're happy with your current configuration, get the most bang for your buck with new paint, a new lighting plan, and maybe even a new floor. If your kitchen needs a full overhaul, consider the following tips to help control costs.

DESIGN

Save money by designing the kitchen yourself with the help of computer software. This is a money-saving choice only if you have the time and capability to plan every detail, both structural and cosmetic. If you aren't comfortable making these decisions and opt not to get professional design help, you may end up spending more to fix your mistakes than you would have by hiring someone in the first place. Another way to save on design costs is to buy your cabinets from a manufacturer that offers free design services. If you need an architect, look for one who's still in school or one who works for a small firm. They will charge less to draw up the plans.

APPLIANCES

Don't get carried away and buy a pro-style range if the most cooking you ever do is boiling water for pasta. You can always upgrade appliances later if you want to, so for now choose less expensive models that will serve the purpose. Be sure that new appliances meet modern energy efficiency standards so they don't end up costing a fortune to run.

MATERIALS

If the countertop material you've chosen is busting the budget, consider using the expensive material on only one run or section of the counter and use a less expensive material like laminate or ceramic tile for the rest. While new cabinets are always expensive, you can save money by choosing stock instead of custom and by opting for one or more large pantry cabinets. This will be less expensive than installing separate upper and lower cabinets in the same space. Fill the space with a pullout wire organizer that you purchase separately.

STICKING TO THE PLAN

Remodeling a kitchen is an expensive project, so naturally you'd like to know how much it will cost as soon as possible. But the only way to accurately compare the bids you'll get from contractors is to come up with a specific plan that includes the design and materials you want. If you don't give enough detailed information, or if you tell different contractors different things, you won't be comparing apples to apples and will likely end up getting bids that are higher than they need to be. Work with a kitchen designer, an architect, or on your own to come up with a clear plan before getting construction bids.

OPPOSITE PAGE: Stock cabinet companies offer the most popular designs and finishes. In a large kitchen like this, choosing stock over custom cabinets can save a lot of money. Ceramic tile on the floor and backsplash adds low-cost color.

Laminate countertops are much less expensive than stone or solid-surface counters. They come in a wide range of colors and patterns and work with any style of kitchen.

When the bids come in, try to resist automatically taking the lowest one. Price alone should not determine whom you hire. Choose the person who you think will do the best job and stay on schedule. Otherwise, you may save a few dollars now but have to spend a lot more later to have shoddy work redone.

Once you have a plan, stick to it. If you change your mind on something even as seemingly minor as where a receptacle should be after construction is under way, you will increase the cost of your project. Before construction begins, make sure that you have studied your final plans and that you are happy with everything from the configuration to the appliances. Then, once construction starts, try not to catch the remodeling bug and decide to do more than you originally planned.

Even if you do stick to your plan, surprises may come up. For example, you might find rot or mold problems that need to be dealt with, or you may need to upgrade your pipes or electrical system once you see their condition inside the walls. It's best to put aside an additional 15 to 25 percent of the total you plan to spend on the remodel to pay for such surprises. That way, you won't end up going over your budget if the unthinkable happens.

KITCHEN STYLE

You may know exactly what you want your new kitchen to look like if you've been dreaming about this project for ages. Or you may never have given kitchen design a thought. The beginning of the project is the time to do your research and think big.

Flip through books and magazines and watch home improvement shows on television. Look at the websites of companies that sell kitchen fixtures and cabinets. Browse appliance stores, custom cabinet showrooms, and home improvement centers. Keep a folder of all the pictures, ideas, and advertisements that catch your eye. Eventually you should start to see a theme emerge. Do the photos you've clipped all have light wood cabinets or stainless steel appliances? Are they of vintage kitchens or sleek and modern spaces? Is there a color scheme you seem to be drawn to?

Take cues from the style and age of your home. If you live in a house built in the late 1800s or early 1900s, consider bringing the kitchen back to its original vintage glory. There are many companies that manufacture new period fixtures that look just like the originals but utilize modern technology. For example, you can get a freestanding range or refrigerator that looks like a period piece but is actually a new product with state-of-the-art features.

LEFT: An apron-front sink with a brass faucet and an open plate rack above give a period look to this kitchen. **BELOW:** Every detail down to the cabinet pulls will help define your kitchen's style.

LEFT: This kitchen, with its marbleized floor and solid-surface countertop, would work just as well in a ranch-style home as it would in a high-rise condominium.
BELOW: Dark-stained cabinets give a traditional air to this kitchen. The warmth of the wood is echoed in the color choices of sage green and golden yellow on the walls.

Classic kitchens work best with classic materials, such as linoleum floors and soapstone countertops. The kitchen of an Arts and Crafts home should feature clean, geometric shapes with contrasting textures and lines. Consider using handmade art tiles for the backsplash in browns and turquoise, dark metals, and dark stained or painted wood cabinets. Modern and Art Deco homes built between 1920 and 1975 should have elegant and simple kitchens with clean lines. They look great with glass-front cabinets, stainless steel appliances, and stone or steel countertops. If you aren't finding enough clues about how kitchens from your style of house used to look from magazines and advertisements, go to the library and look at photos from that era or check out some architecture books.

If your house has no discernable architectural style, then choose whatever kind of kitchen that appeals to you, from Country French to eclectic.

COLOR

The colors you choose for the walls, floors, cabinets, countertop, and backsplash should be harmonious. Try to limit the number of colors in the kitchen to three—one that is most dominant, one that is secondary, and one used as an accent. Cool or light colors will make a small space seem bigger, while warm, dark, or bright colors tend to visually shrink the room. You'll get the most mileage out of neutral-colored cabinets and flooring that could be made to work with a variety of styles in years to come. Consider stained wood or white cabinets and a neutral-colored floor, and then use the backsplash, lighting fixtures, and accessories to add some personal style to the room.

Put together a sample design board where you can display examples of the colors and materials you're considering for the kitchen. Include paint chips, samples of your countertop choice, pictures of the appliances, and pieces of the flooring. If the colors and textures all seem to work together on the board, chances are they'll look good on a much larger scale as well. Be sure to check out the colors on the sample board under the kitchen lights at night and by natural light during the day. If you aren't sure about the paint color, buy a 4-by-5-foot piece of foam core board, paint it with the color you're considering, and hold that up in various areas of the room. This will give you a more realistic look at the color than a paint chip will.

OPPOSITE PAGE: These European-style cabinets with a glossy red finish and continuous aluminum pulls make quite a color statement in this modern kitchen. **ABOVE:** Cream-colored thermofoil cabinets are an elegant backdrop to colorful glass backsplash tiles. **RIGHT:** When it comes to color, don't overlook the kitchen sink. Porcelain-coated sinks like this one come in a variety of colors to match every palette.

CHOOSING CABINETS

Selecting and ordering new cabinets for your kitchen remodel is a time-consuming and often confusing process. Should you go with stock or custom? Face-frame or frameless? Glass or solid doors? Because new cabinets are a big invest-ment—often costing up to half of what you'll spend on the entire remodel—it's important to get it right so you'll end up with an arrangement that meets your storage needs and that comple-ments the design of your new kitchen.

STOCK, SEMI-CUSTOM, OR CUSTOM

The decision of whether to buy off-the-shelf, semi-custom, or custom cabinets depends on your budget, how important it is to have an original design or finish, the size of your kitchen, and how long you can wait for them to arrive.

While the colors and styles available used to be somewhat limited, these days stock cabinet compa-nies offer many features that people choose custom cabinets for, such as integrated moldings and full-extension drawer glides. Stock companies also carry the most popular styles, so it's likely they'll offer something that fits your needs. These cabinets are made in widths starting at 9 inches and increasing in 3-inch increments, maxing out at 48 inches wide. You can get filler pieces so the cabinet boxes look like they reach all the way to the wall. Unless you have an odd-shaped kitchen or need to maxi-mize every inch, these set meas-urements should work for you. And if your remodel is on a tight schedule, you'll appreciate the fact that stock cabinets can be deliv-ered to your door about one to two weeks after you order them.

A less expensive option is RTA (ready-to-assemble) cabinets,

Choosing a cohesive cabinet arrange-ment that meets your storage needs, works with the style of your home, and doesn't break the bank can be a challenge. But your research can result in a gorgeous finished kitchen, as these white and stained wood semi-custom cabinets show.

LEFT: Face-frame cabinets with partial overlay doors are more traditional and show the cabinet box. **BELOW:** Frameless (European-style) cabinets feature doors that completely cover the cabinet box.

FACE-FRAME OR FRAMELESS

The definitions of face-frame and frameless cabinets can devolve into a confusing and academic argument, so we'll keep it simple. With face-frame cabinets, you can see the rails and stiles around the cabinet doors. With frameless (often referred to as European style), all you see are the doors. Face-frame cabinets look good in traditional or vintage-style kitchens, while frameless cabinets work well in more sleek and contemporary kitchens. Beyond style, frameless cabinets offer more interior space, as the entire cabinet box is accessible, while the frames of face-frame cabinets can make getting large items through the door openings more difficult.

which come flattened in a box, and are cheaper only if you don't have to hire someone to assemble and install them for you.

Semi-custom cabinets are also made in factories with some mass-produced components, but the manufacturers offer custom sizes and finishes. The cost can be about 30 percent more than stock, but you'll have more choices and can maximize the storage space in your kitchen. If your heart is set on a specific wood type or configuration, you may be able to find a semi-custom solution.

Choose custom cabinets if you want an original design, need to use every inch of an odd-sized space, or prefer to work one-on-one with a smaller and more personalized company. Depending on where you live, some custom cabinets are quite competitively priced, so don't rule them out without getting a few bids. Be sure to factor in enough lead-time—some custom cabinet shops need two or more months to complete an order.

A glaze finish emphasizes the grooves in paneled doors.

DOOR STYLES

Doors come in dozens of styles. They can be flat (or slab), they can have one or more raised or recessed panels that are either straight-edged or curved, and they can evoke certain styles depending on how wide or narrow the outside profile is. The door you choose will make a strong impact and help to define the overall style of your kitchen, so make sure you see all your choices before making a decision. Beyond the style of door, you'll need to decide among inset doors, which sit flush with the cabinet box; partial overlay doors, which rest on top of the face frame; or full overlay doors, which practically touch one another. If you want to visually open up the space or if you feel overwhelmed by large spans of wood cabinets, consider glass-front doors with either clear, etched, ribbed, frosted, or colored glass.

MATERIALS AND CRAFTSMANSHIP

Most wood cabinets are not constructed exclusively of hardwood. The cabinet box is usually made of medium-density fiberboard (MDF) or plywood either left bare or covered with wood veneer. The reason for this is partly cost and partly practicality. Wood expands and contracts depending on the room's temperature and humidity levels, and this movement could wreak havoc on your joints and finishes. If the way your cabinets look on the inside matters to you, or if you plan to have glass doors, order them with interior wood veneer that matches the color and variety on the doors and cabinet face. Popular wood choices for kitchen cabinets include maple, oak, pine, alder, and cherry, though custom shops can make them out of practically anything. Painted cabinets and doors are often made of MDF rather than solid wood, allowing for a smoother and more even finish. Other choices are thermofoil (a vinyl material applied over MDF), or melamine, which is made of particleboard covered with laminate.

Drawer faces and doors are made of either solid wood, plywood, or MDF. Drawers whose face also acts as the fourth side of the drawer box are less sturdy than drawers that have four sides and a separate front piece. Look for ball-bearing or track-and-roller drawer hardware that can handle heavy loads and that opens and closes smoothly and quietly.

These doors sit flush with the cabinet box.

ABOVE: Frosted glass door inserts allow you to see colors but hide the clutter. These doors include a thick aluminum frame for a modern look. RIGHT: Slab doors don't have to be plain, as these glossy wood-grained cabinets prove.

TIPS | DIY Network
Home Improvement

PULLS AND KNOBS

Here's where you get to add some personality to your cabinets. Choose milk glass or crystal knobs for vintage-style kitchens, frosted glass, or sleek chrome for modern kitchens, square antique bronze pulls for Arts and Crafts kitchens, or knobs shaped like peas and carrots for eclectic kitchens. Before you get carried away, though, think about whether children or people with reduced hand strength will be using the kitchen. If so, stay away from pulls that are sharp or awkwardly shaped, and opt instead for wide pulls with smooth edges.

CHOOSING COUNTERTOPS

You may be tempted to choose your kitchen countertop based on looks alone. After all, it's a highly visible part of the kitchen and the material and color you choose will have a big impact on the overall design. But the countertop must also work for your daily needs, so take the time to weigh the pros and cons of each material before deciding which is right for your kitchen.

SOLID-SURFACE

Sold under many brand names, solid-surface countertops are popular for their durability and for the range of available colors and patterns. They are extremely malleable and can be formed into practically anything, so if you want an island shaped like a question mark, this would be a good choice for the countertop. Seams are invisible, and you can remove minor cuts and scratches by sanding the surface as the color goes all the way through. Easy to clean and nonporous, it can handle anything except a scorching hot pan. So if you tend to put your hot pans on the countertop, have metal strips installed on top of the counter next to the range, or have a hot pad on hand. Solid-surface countertops must be installed by a professional.

LAMINATE

Made of thin layers of kraft paper and melamine plastic bound by heat and pressure, laminate is available in hundreds of colors and patterns. Some of the darker colors in high sheens can even mimic the look of stone. Laminate countertops longer than 12 feet will have visible seams. Make sure you keep any seams well sealed so that water doesn't seep in, curl the edges, and damage the countertop. Consider spending the extra money for color-core laminate, which has color under the surface. Scratches will be better hidden that way. Laminate is less durable than solid-surface and will melt under very hot pans. It's a good choice if you have a tight budget or want to do a quick makeover and possibly upgrade to a different kind of counter in a few years.

TOP LEFT: Solid surface countertops
LEFT: Laminate countertop surface

RIGHT: Soapstone countertop surface

CERAMIC TILE

Available in almost any shape and color imaginable, tile is a durable, heat-resistant, water-resistant choice for a kitchen countertop. Choose tiles that are flat and even so you can set glasses on the counter without them falling over. Smooth tiles are also easier to clean. Tiles should be rated for countertop use. Decorative and glass tiles aren't sturdy enough to withstand having objects dropped on them and are better choices for the backsplash. Install countertop tiles over a base of plywood topped with cement backerboard. Adhere the tile to the backerboard with mastic instead of thinset, as mastic is more flexible. Epoxy grout will resist stains and mildew better than regular grout, but it's still a good idea to seal the grout yearly.

STONE

Most high-end kitchens feature stone countertops, whether granite, marble, or limestone. Remember that each batch of quarried stone can take on different colors and patterns, so the sample piece you see in the store may not be what you end up getting. If possible, buy your kitchen countertop from a stone yard that allows you to pick your own slab. Usually, a stone counter longer than 9 feet will have a seam. Stone is also very heavy, so make sure your cabinets and subfloor are strong enough to support the weight.

While nothing beats the natural beauty of stone, it's not always the best choice for kitchens that get a lot of heavy use. Granite is the most durable, heat-resistant, and scratch-resistant. But all stone is porous, and granite will need to be sealed with an impregnator at least once a year. Pastry chefs love marble countertops because they stay cool for kneading dough. Even after it's sealed, marble can be stained if oil, alcohol, or acids such as lemon juice sit on the counter for several hours. If your heart is set on marble, check regularly to see if a bead of water creates a dark spot when left for more than 10 minutes, and seal it every few months to avoid stains. Even with these precautions, though, you'll have to wipe up spills immediately and never cut directly on the stone. Limestone will require similar diligence. Slate is naturally water-resistant and comes in many colors and textures (it's not all gray). It should be sealed once a year. Soapstone is less porous than slate, making it a highly durable choice in the world of natural stone. Spills wipe up easily, it won't burn or stain, and it can even be used for an integral sink. All soapstone is a dark charcoal color with white veins throughout.

STAINLESS STEEL

Kitchens in restaurants and hospitals use stainless steel countertops because they are hygienic and easy to clean. This type of counter also looks great in sleek and modern residential kitchens. Buy the thickest steel you can afford—16 gauge minimum or lower (the lower the gauge, the thicker the steel). A ¾-inch plywood substrate installed under a thick layer of steel will help quiet this noisy material. Consider adding an integrated stainless steel sink or having the steel run in one piece from the backsplash to the counter's edge, but remember that a stretch of steel more than 9 feet long will require a visible seam. Steel resists water and heat, but it scratches easily. Most people consider those fine scratches to be part of the charm and don't worry about them. Wipe up water quickly to avoid water marks.

QUARTZ

This manmade stone can take whatever you throw at it and will never need sealing. It's nonporous, and it resists stains, heat, and scratches. Quartz is available in many colors and can be custom ordered in non-standard sizes. Unlike natural stone, what you see in the showroom is exactly what you'll get.

CLOCKWISE FROM TOP: Stainless steel, quartz, butcher block

WOOD

Butcher-block counters are usually made of laminated maple, but you can choose from a wide range of hardwood types. Wood is a great choice for islands or chopping areas, as it is a natural cutting board. While beautiful, wood needs regular maintenance to keep it looking its best. It should be cleaned and dried every day, then rubbed with a nontoxic oil (like mineral, walnut,

Concrete countertop surface

or raw tung oil) every few weeks to hydrate the wood and prevent cracks. Use it alone or in conjunction with another countertop material.

◀ CONCRETE ▶

This durable material is stain-resistant and easy to keep clean when properly sealed. Concrete looks great in modern homes, and because it can be colored and decorative accents can be embedded in the counter, it works in any style of kitchen. In addition to sealing, it's a good idea to wax the concrete every few months. The counter can be pre-cast off site or cast in place, which is quite labor-intensive and therefore expensive. Be sure to hire someone with lots of experience in this field, because if the countertop doesn't end up looking good, it will be a huge pain to get rid of. Like stone, this is a heavy countertop, so be sure your cabinets and floor can take the weight.

BACKSPLASH

The backsplash is a good place to splurge on decorative tiles, glass mosaics, or copper. It can be as little as 4 inches high, but it's wise to protect the wall all the way up to the bottom of the upper cabinets. If you prefer to see the wall, be sure it's painted with scrubbable satin or glossy paint. Relief tiles or those that are too bumpy to use on the countertop give texture to the backsplash. Consider running less expensive field tiles on most of the wall and using the art tiles sparingly if you're trying to keep costs down. Whatever kind of tile you use, make sure the horizontal grout lines match the wall cabinets and countertops or else the wall will look slanted. Use silicone acrylic caulk where the backsplash tiles and the counter meet, as grout there will crack.

The key to an organized kitchen storage system is to keep items in the proper location. Cooking utensils should be near the cooktop. Everyday dishes and glasses should be near the dishwasher. Dishes and appliances you rarely use should be kept on the top shelves of overhead cabinets. Take the time to think about how you use your kitchen and what you need to store, and then choose storage accessories like the ones shown here to help make your kitchen run like a well-oiled machine.

ABOVE: Deep pullout drawers can store pots and pans, pantry items, and even plates. Various inserts keep everything in its place. BELOW: Hide trash and recyclables in a base cabinet equipped with heavy-duty hardware.

Hang cooking spices and utensils from a metal rod that spans the backsplash above your range so that everything you need is right at hand. Keep in mind, though, that close proximity to high heat can diminish the quality of your spices over time.

LEFT: Baking sheets, spices, and cooking utensils are kept in the cabinets on either side of this range, while pots that are used frequently hang from hooks on a metal pegboard (see page 94 to learn how to make your own). ABOVE: Utensils stay separated with a built-in wood organizer, and knives in individually-sized holders on their own tray slide out of your way. BELOW: This simple wine rack built into a kitchen cabinet can store up to 40 bottles.

TIPS | DIY Network
Home Improvement

SPACE-SAVING IDEAS

Cookie sheets, muffin tins, and cutting boards can be stored vertically in a tall, narrow cabinet.

Baking supplies such as flour and whole grains can be kept in drawers outfitted with plastic canisters.

Pullout metal racks can be used for everything from pantry staples to cleaning supplies.

Short or tall pantry cabinets can be outfitted with a variety of pullout drawers and wire shelves. Racks can be attached to the backs of doors to hold small bottles and packages.

Put a tiered rack in an upper cabinet so you can see contents all the way in the back.

APPLIANCES

One or more new appliances can make a huge impact in your kitchen. If you've been limping along with a dishwasher that will clean only hand-scrubbed dishes, a refrigerator that leaks, or an oven whose temperature never quite works with the recipe you're using, you will be amazed at what modern appliances have to offer.

Before you buy, make sure the new appliances will fit through your door and in the same spot as the old appliances if you're not also getting new cabinets. Some appliance manufacturers now offer smaller than standard-size ranges, dishwashers, and refrigerators for homes with small kitchens. If you don't cook much and live alone or with one other person, these smaller appliances may be all you need and will give you more counter space. On the other side of the spectrum, people with large kitchens who are looking for mammoth ranges with six or more burners, or industrial-size refrigerators, should make sure that their kitchen's subfloor will hold the extra weight.

Beyond the basics, there are specialty appliances on the market that can personalize your kitchen. Built-in pizza ovens and espresso machines give you professional results in the comfort of your own home. Warming drawers keep food warm without cooking it. Set them as low as 90 degrees to warm plates for Sunday morning pancakes, or as high as 250 degrees to keep soup hot for a late-working spouse. Under-counter coolers with fine-tuned temperature controls are specially designed for keeping wine collections chilled to perfection. For these and any new appliance, it's best to shop in person to make sure you are comfortable with the setup and controls. Be sure to compare prices both in stores and online, as they can vary by hundreds of dollars. But also take delivery and shipping charges into account before making a decision.

LEFT: Modern dishwashers often have hidden controls on the top edge of the door; this allows you to choose decorative faces to match your cabinets or other appliances.
OPPOSITE PAGE: This side-by-side refrigerator sits flush with the cabinets and includes a through-the-door ice maker.

also choose stainless steel or glass doors), and has no ventilation gaps in the front, making it quiet and unobtrusive. Integrated models come in a range of sizes, so even though they are shallower than free-standing refrigerators, you can get the cubic footage you need. The general guideline is to allow 10 cubic feet of refrigerator space for two people, and 1.5 cubic feet more for each additional person.

Under-counter refrigerators and freezers are becoming popular in large kitchens where it's more convenient to have some items nearer the area they will be used, such as storing fruits and vegetables next to the prep sink. These are generally used in addition to a standard refrigerator-freezer, but if you don't keep much frozen food, you might consider buying a refrigerator without a built-in freezer and having an under-counter freezer in a separate location.

DISHWASHERS

Great strides have been made in modern dishwash-ers. They are quiet and energy efficient, and some even have built-in disposals so you don't have to rinse the dishes before putting them in the machine. Models with low energy consumption and the option of lighter washes for half-full loads save water and money. Some can heat the water to 140 degrees before the cycle begins instead of depending on your home's hot-water tank, which may not have enough hot water to accommodate the dishwasher every time you use it. This feature will sterilize your dishes more effectively. The standard size dishwasher is 24 inches wide, 24 inches deep, and 34 inches high, but you can find compact models that are 18 inches wide. Consider installing two dishwashers if you have a large family, like to entertain, or keep kosher. There are also dishwashers that come as two deep drawers so that you can wash fine stemware on one setting and large pans on another.

REFRIGERATORS

Freestanding models are available with side-by-side refrigerator and freezer areas, a freezer on top and refrigerator on the bottom, or the freezer on the bottom as one or two pullout drawers. A side-by-side configuration allows the option of a through-the-door ice dispenser, but larger items can sometimes be tough to fit inside. If you shop in bulk or eat a lot of large frozen pizzas, you may prefer a top or bottom freezer configuration instead. Freestanding models can stick out as much as 8 inches past your countertop. Built-in models stick out past the cabi-nets only slightly, and they can accept cabinet panels so that the refrigerator will blend in with the rest of the kitchen. But the only way for the refrigerator to truly disappear into a run of cabinets is to buy an integrated model, which sits completely flush with the cabinets, takes cabinet panels (although you can

RANGES

A range is a cooktop and oven in one, and models can be either freestanding or built into a run of cabinets. They operate on gas, electricity, and dual fuel, which combines an electric oven with gas burners. Standard width is 30 inches, but you can find models as narrow as 21 inches and as wide as 48 inches. Beware of commercial ranges for home use, as they get very hot to the touch and are often too heavy for home subfloors. If you like the commercial range look, choose one of the pro-style models that offer similar power and size but are lighter, safer, and easier to keep clean. There are many cooktop types with a variety of features such as griddle plates and wok burners. Some cooktops have built-in vents so there's no need for a separate vent hood. There are also lots of options for the oven portion of the range, including convection ovens, which cook food faster and more evenly.

COOKTOPS AND OVENS

A cooktop can be placed separate from the oven, which is preferable in some kitchen designs. A separate oven makes sense if you don't want to stoop

Stand-alone ranges offer extra kitchen layout options

Cooktop surface

down to put things in and take things out of a range oven, or if you want two ovens or an oven/warming drawer combination. In these cases, put the oven(s) at shoulder height in one location and the cooktop in another. Cooktops are usually 30 inches wide for four burners and get wider as you add more burners. Pay attention to the burner BTU ratings of the models you're considering. Standard burners go from a low of about 2,000 BTU to a high of 12,000 BTU. Some pro-style models offer 15,000 or more BTU on one burner to boil water quickly, and burners that can go as low as 400 BTU for keeping sauces warm.

When shopping for an oven, you'll have a choice of gas or electric (though electric is far more common), as well as a choice of the kind of heat used. Conventional ovens use radiant heat, while convection ovens cook food faster by using a high-speed fan that circulates heated air. Convection ovens can cook a main course and a dessert at the same time with no transfer of flavors. Look for options such as browning and thawing, combination convection/radiant heat, ovens that can also be used as microwaves and, of course, self-cleaning features. Built-in ovens are made to fit within 24-inch-deep cabinets. Compact ovens for small kitchens are available, but some are too small to fit a standard-size cookie sheet, so consider the interior measurements before you buy.

MICROWAVES

A full kitchen remodel is a great opportunity to find space for a built-in microwave rather than having one that takes up valuable counter space. Put the microwave in a spot where children and shorter adults can reach it. Right above or right below the counter is a good choice, as you will have a spot to put hot dishes nearby.

Built-in microwaves save valuable countertop space

VENTILATION

While not as exciting as shopping for a new dishwasher or range, making sure you have proper ventilation in the kitchen is crucial. All the fumes, moisture, and grease generated from the cooktop can damage the surfaces of your kitchen, and even your entire house, if left to linger in the air. A vent hood placed over the cooktop will draw in odors and grease and release them outside. The fan is connected to a series of ducts that run through your walls and out the nearest location, such as through an exterior wall or the roof. Short spans of ventilation piping, which are made of rigid galvanized metal, are most efficient. If the vent pipes must make turns, use two 45-degree turns rather than one 90-degree turn. Make sure the vent hood is powerful enough for the size of your cooktop. A general rule is to have at least 40 CFM (cubic feet per minute of air displacement) per linear foot of cooktop. The vent pipe can be covered with upper cabinets or a decorative hood. If you'd prefer not to have an overhead vent hood for aesthetic reasons, or your cooktop is on an island and a hood would visually disrupt the room, buy a downdraft vent that pops up from behind your cooktop when needed.

SINKS AND FAUCETS

There are many designs, sizes, and finishes available in kitchen sinks and faucets. Choose a combination that works with the style of your kitchen, that is comfortable for you to use, and that is easy to keep clean.

◢ SINKS ◣

Sinks come in a wide variety of sizes, shapes, depths, and configurations. First decide whether you prefer a drop-in (also called self-rimming) or undermount sink. Drop-in sinks are most common and have a lip that sits on top of the counter. It's a more traditional look, but when you wipe the counter, crumbs can collect around the edges of the sink. Undermount sinks allow you to wipe counter contents straight into the sink, which is attached under the counter with metal clips. These models have a more sleek and modern look but can work in any style of kitchen. A third choice is an integral sink, which is molded out of the same piece of solid-surface material as the countertop. Make sure you pick a sink with the right number of pre-drilled holes for your faucet and any accessories you want, like a sprayer.

Think about how you use your kitchen sink to decide on how many bowls you need. If you clean a lot of large pots and pans, you may prefer one large bowl. Double bowls are useful if you tend to stack dirty dishes in the sink. You can put them in the larger bowl and still use the smaller bowl to rinse food. The garbage disposal is usually installed in the smaller bowl. Three-bowl sinks often have two large bowls on each side for cleaning or stacking dishes, and one small bowl in the middle for food prep.

ABOVE LEFT: Double-bowl undermount sink. LEFT: Single-bowl drop-in sink. BELOW: Triple-bowl sink with cutting board accessory.

ABOVE: Widespread faucet. RIGHT: Centerset faucet with pull-out spray nozzle.

Look for a sink with an offset drain, which allows more flat space for stacking dishes and lets water drain even if a large pot is soaking in the center. Other handy features include integrated cutting boards and dish-drying racks.

Common sink materials include stainless steel, enameled cast iron, vitreous china, and solid surface. Stainless steel is hygienic and attractive but easy to scratch, and the sound of water hitting the sink can be surprisingly loud. The thicker the metal, the quieter it is. Buy at least 16-gauge steel—the lower the gauge, the thicker the metal. Also check that there is foam insulation under the sink, which absorbs the sound of water and dishes hitting it. Enameled cast iron is a hard, smooth surface that's available in lots of colors. It's very quiet and easy to keep clean, but it can chip if something heavy falls on it. Vitreous china is a molded clay that's been fired at high temperature. It comes in decorative shapes, can be found with painted designs, and is easy to clean, but it also can chip. Solid-surface sinks are usually integral with the countertop, but you can find them as stand-alone sinks as well. They are durable and come in lots of colors. As with a solid-surface countertop, you can repair the sink if it gets scratched or stained.

FAUCETS

Choosing between a centerset and widespread faucet is a matter of personal taste. Centerset faucets can be worked with one hand, so some people find them easier to use when hands are dirty or soapy. They are also easier for people with reduced hand strength. Widespread faucets have separate hot and cold handles and have a more traditional look. The most important thing in a faucet is that it have solid-brass workings and ceramic disc valves so that it is drip free and long lasting. In general, the heavier the faucet, the better it's made.

Make sure the faucet you choose will be compatible with your sink. If your sink has more holes than your faucet needs, it should have filler pieces to cover them up. Don't match a huge faucet with a small sink or vice versa. Otherwise water may spray back at you or not reach every corner of the sink. Also, if you have a window over your sink, make sure the faucet is short enough to fit under the windowsill. Check those dimensions before making a purchase.

Some manufacturers offer safety features that limit how hot the water can get, which can be helpful when children are using the faucet. Finish choices for kitchen faucets include polished and brushed chrome, polished and antique brass, and powder-coat enamel.

FLOORING

Whatever flooring material you decide to go with, make sure that it's comfortable to stand on for long periods, that it's not terribly slippery when wet, and that it's easy to keep clean. Most types of flooring are suitable for the kitchen, so choose what you like and what works with the design of the room.

ABOVE: Slate. ABOVE RIGHT: Vinyl tile

VINYL

Vinyl flooring is a popular choice for the kitchen. It's relatively simple to install (especially if you have a flat and sound subfloor), it resists water damage, it's available in textures that are slip-resistant, and it's one of the least expensive options. It does require some basic upkeep, though. If you don't buy prewaxed vinyl, then you should seal it regularly. If the edges aren't sealed, water can seep in and damage your subfloor. Some vinyl can discolor when exposed to sunlight, and some can be easily punctured by sharp objects or heavy furniture.

CERAMIC TILE

Tile is a durable flooring material for the kitchen because it's naturally resistant to water and stains. It comes in an incredible array of colors and shapes. Large floor tiles with fewer grout lines are preferable in the kitchen, as they are easier to keep clean. Tiles with a slight texture are less slippery if you spill something on the floor. Be sure to seal the grout so it doesn't stain.

STONE

An elegant, high-end choice, stone works beautifully in the kitchen and can be well worth the high price.

Pick a textured or honed stone finish rather than a smooth and glossy one for better slip resistance. Seal it to keep out moisture and dirt. Marble can be cold and slippery, and it's heavy enough that you'll need to be sure your subfloor can take the weight. Slate is naturally textured and water-resistant, making it a good choice for the kitchen.

WOOD

Wood can't be beat for a warm, comfortable look, and it's soft underfoot. If you have hardwood floors in the rest of your house, consider carrying them through to the new kitchen. Wood can be damaged by moisture and spills, so be sure your hardwood kitchen floor is well sealed at all times. A lower-maintenance alternative is a laminate or engineered wood floor, which comes prefinished and factory sealed and is less susceptible to water damage.

RESILIENT

Natural materials such as linoleum and cork fall under this category. Linoleum is resistant to bacteria and has antistatic properties that repel dust and grime, making it an excellent choice for the kitchen. Cork is anti-microbial but not water-resistant and needs to be kept sealed. Both are quiet and warm underfoot.

CONCRETE

Concrete is fast becoming a popular choice in modern and contemporary homes. It's obviously hard to damage, and it's easy to clean. Decorative concrete techniques can be utilized for color and pattern. Its downsides are that it's cold and hard on your feet, though you can install a radiant in-floor heat system underneath to warm it up. Concrete should be sealed regularly to repel stains.

LEFT: Hardwood. ABOVE: Concrete

LIGHTING

If you've been making do with one overhead light in your kitchen, it's time for an upgrade. Sometimes just a new lighting plan and a coat of paint can make all the difference in a drab kitchen.

ABOVE: A downlight pendant hangs over the kitchen island, while lights under the vent hood illuminate the cooktop area. ABOVE RIGHT: Use a variety of lighting, such as recessed lights, ceiling fixtures, and pendants.

A single light source in a kitchen means that you're doing most of your work in the shadows. Bright kitchens are more inviting and safer to work in. If you're not sure how to update the lighting plan in your kitchen, consider hiring a lighting designer who will come to your house and assess your needs. Or you can take your kitchen drawings to a local lighting store. Sometimes the store will offer free design services and help you figure out a balanced lighting plan for the room.

Draw out where each light will go and which switch will operate it. It's best to have ambient and task lighting on separate switches so they can be operated independently. Also check your local building codes. In an effort to lower energy consumption, some states now require that kitchen remodels include a certain percentage of energy-efficient fluorescent lights. Darker surfaces will require about 50 percent more light than white kitchens, so choosing lighter cabinets and floors will actually save money on your electric bill.

Very small kitchens can sometimes get by with one overhead lighting source and under-cabinet lighting, but most kitchens need a combination of ambient, task, and accent lighting. Ceiling fixtures and recessed lights spaced evenly around the room can provide ambient light, while recessed downlights and pendants provide task lighting over the stove and sink. Fluorescent tubes are the best choice to illuminate the countertops under wall cabinets. They provide even, shadowless light. Most wall cabinets don't reach all the way to the ceiling, leaving dark areas at the top of the walls. Use track lights on top of the wall cabinets to illuminate these areas, which will make the entire room seem larger.

Kitchen offices and workspaces also need task lighting. If your kitchen is part of a great room or eating area, make sure the lighting blends from one room to the next so you aren't hit with a harsh light the minute you step into the kitchen. Using the same color bulbs throughout the kitchen, and in adjoining spaces, will ensure that the tone of each surface has the same intensity.

RIGHT: This ceiling fixture has a vintage look, which ties in nicely with the wainscot and retro clock. BELOW: Install under-cabinet task lights to avoid working in the shadows.

TIPS | DIY Network
Home Improvement

TRACK LIGHTING

Look for new track lighting systems with curved rods that allow you to point light right where you want it. The lights can also be moved to another part of the rod if your needs change. It's a quick and easy way to add task lighting to any kitchen.

Weekend Kitchen Makeovers

2

Projects

These 11 kitchen projects are some of my favorites from the show. Some are complete renovations, while others are "48-hour makeovers," where quick and easy changes made all the difference.

What I've tried to do is to give you a step-by-step recap of the techniques that made a huge impact on the final design aspects of these kitchens. Some of these techniques are general to kitchen design and you can substitute the materials with your own. But other methods are specific to the products we used, so make sure to double-check the installation instructions that come with your materials.

Keep in mind that you have to pace yourself with these projects. Many can be done in a short amount of time, while others will take significantly longer. Even simple projects can take a lot of time from start to finish. For example, the paint has to dry before you can install those cabinet doors, the drywall compound has to set before you can sand it, and so on.

Finally, keep the instructions, owner's manuals, and any other reference materials that come with the particular products you intend to install. Start a folder that is easily accessible so you can go back and double-check facts and figures along the way.

Now let's get busy!

Paul

diy
network
MOM'S KITCHEN

Mom needed a new kitchen, so my equally handy brothers and I pitched in to give our mother the kitchen of her dreams. We gutted the entire space, pulling out 1960's metal cabinets, four layers of linoleum, and dingy-looking white countertops. In its place, a traditional kitchen with vintage charm emerged.

BEFORE: This retro white kitchen was showing its age.

AFTER: Maple cabinets and a slate countertop really warmed up the space.

◀ PROJECT SUMMARY ▶

We installed industrial-grade vinyl tile on the floor in a two-color diamond pattern. Then semi-custom maple cabinets with a combination of cognac and garnet finishes were installed. The upper cabinets are a little lower on the wall than standard so that Mom can reach them without a stool. A three-tiered crown molding arrangement on top makes them seem closer to the ceiling. A large range hood covered in garnet beadboard houses a new 700-CFM vent system. Under-cabinet lighting brightens up the rich green, honed, Vermont slate countertops. Butcher-block counters flank the freestanding range. Above the range, Mom's old pegboard organizer got an update in the form of a perforated steel backsplash. She used to keep her calendar and phone on the kitchen counter, but now she can use a new built-in desk in the breakfast nook.

A coat of paint on the walls, new cabinet hardware, a built-in microwave, and new stainless steel and black appliances tie the whole look together.

Old meets new, from the classic vinyl floor to the stainless steel appliances to the crown molding details.

The beadboard vent hood serves as a focal point over the range.

A

B

C

D

◀ INSTALLING UNDERLAYMENT ▶

Before installing the new underlayment, make sure the subfloor is as smooth and clean as possible. Remove every remaining staple and sweep up all debris.

1 Lay out full sheets of underlayment (photo A). Use the type that has printed X's on it, which show you where to staple each sheet into the subfloor so you're sure to use the recommended number of staples.

2 Mark the areas that need cutouts and use a jigsaw to make the cuts.

3 For a professional look, you want your underlayment and flooring to fit under the doorjamb rather than wrap around it. Use a piece of underlayment and a floor tile for spacing to determine how much of the jamb to remove. Lay a power jamb saw or a Japanese pull saw (photo B) on top of these pieces while you make the cut, and you'll remove enough of the jamb to allow for the thickness of the finished floor.

4 Secure the underlayment to the subfloor with a pneumatic stapler, using 1⅜-inch quarter crown staples that will penetrate into the subfloor by at least an inch. Since the plan is to install vinyl flooring over this underlayment, it's especially important that the surface be smooth. Any bumps will be visible in the finished floor. Pound down the staples with a hammer so they're flush with the surface.

5 Fill the seams by troweling on a thin layer of gypsum-based skim coat (photo C).

6 After about 15 minutes, the gypsum skim coat will be dry. Go over the seams with an orbital sander, smoothing out the high points and feathering the edges (photo D).

You Will Need

- Safety glasses
- Pliers
- Underlayment
- Hammer
- Tape measure
- Jigsaw
- Pneumatic stapler
- Jamb or Japanese pull saw
- 1⅜" quarter crown staples
- Gypsum-based skim coat
- Trowel
- Random orbital sander

You Will Need

Vinyl composite tiles	Premixed adhesive
Vinyl tile cutter	Utility knife
Speed square	100-pound roller
1/32" V-notched trowel	Carpenter's square
Chalk line	Sealant

INSTALLING VINYL COMPOSITE TILE

Vinyl composite floor tiles in a checkerboard pattern set at an angle provide a classic look in this kitchen. To create a symmetrical pattern, make sure the tops of the diamonds will line up straight across the room.

1 Make a perfect 45-degree angle for a starting line. Do this by first finding a 90-degree angle using the rule of 3-4-5. This rule says a triangle with sides of 3 feet, 4 feet, and 5 feet creates a perfect 90-degree angle (diagram A, below). Snap chalk lines and then mark where they intersect for the 90-degree angle (photo A).

2 Use the 90-degree angle to create a new triangle with two sides of equal length to get a 45-degree angle and make a starting line for the tile (diagram B, below, and photo B).

3 Lay out a few rows of the pattern against the starting line. Then move them along that line until the pattern is in the right spot on the floor—in this case, lined up with the doorway (photo C). Before lifting up the tiles to put down the adhesive, mark where the first tile will be placed.

4 Apply the recommended tile adhesive using a 1/32-inch V-notched trowel (photo D), which will leave a minimal amount of glue on

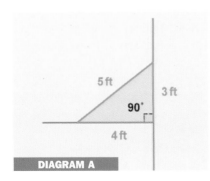

DIAGRAM A

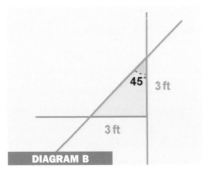

DIAGRAM B

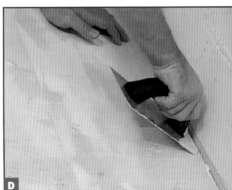

E

F

the underlayment but still provide full coverage. Once the adhesive is applied, it turns clear. You don't want it to skin over in the bucket.

5 Make sure the tiles are clean and start on your mark, setting the tile on the reference line (photo E). Take your time to make sure you have perfect alignment. The tiles stick on contact but can be adjusted. Work your way around the room, kneeling carefully on freshly placed tiles as you go.

6 Make necessary cuts with a vinyl tile cutter (photo F). Simply mark your tile and use a speed square as a guide for a straight cut. Use a utility knife and a carpenter's square if you need to cut a size that won't fit into the tile cutter. If the tiles are tough to cut through, try warming them up first with a heat gun or hair dryer.

7 Once all the tiles are in place, run a 100-pound roller (available at tool rental centers) over the floor a few times. The roller is necessary to ensure that the tiles are all adhering to the underlayment and to provide a smooth finish.

8 Apply a sealer to the finished floor so that dust and debris won't work their way into the seams between the tiles.

INSTALLING THE CABINETS

On top of the upper cabinets is a three-piece stacked molding—a detail rail, a piece of 1-by, and crown on top of that—to add about 10 inches to the top of the cabinets. The detail rail needs to be attached to the upper cabinets before they are installed on the wall. Then the 1-by and crown pieces are added later.

You Will Need

- Safety glasses
- Clamps
- 1¼" cabinet screws
- 2" cabinet screws
- Drill
- Compound miter saw
- Level
- Finish nailer
- Tape measure
- Jigsaw

1 Join the corner bank of cabinets together with clamps. Make pilot holes and use 1¼-inch cabinet screws to fasten the back pieces together (photo A).

2 Next, make pilot holes and secure the face frames together with 2-inch cabinet screws (photo B).

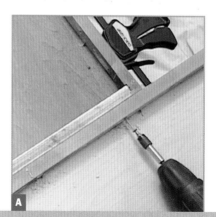

A

B

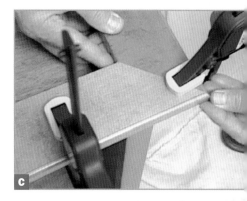

TIPS | DIY Network Home Improvement

SCREWS
Don't use drywall screws for cabinets. They aren't strong enough and will rust over time.

3 Use a compound miter saw to cut the detail rail to fit the cabinet tops. Clamp the rail to the top of the cabinets and make sure you have a uniform reveal all around the top (photo C). This will ensure that the detail sticks out farther than the cabinet doors. Use a finish nailer to secure the detail rail.

4 To hang the upper cabinets, mark the studs on the wall. Hold the cabinet in place and make sure it's level. Then screw the cabinets into the studs.

5 To install the base cabinets, first remove the doors. Use clamps to hold the cabinets together, then drill pilot holes and screw the boxes together.

6 Once the face frames are attached to each other, move the cabinets into position against the wall. Make sure the cabinets are level front to back and side to side. Use shims under the cabinet, if needed, and to fill the gap between the wall and cabinet. Screw a shim against the wall into place (photo D) and then break off the excess. Screw the cabinets into the wall studs.

7 To create a furniture look for the sink cabinet, two decorative bun feet may be added to the front. Flip the sink cabinet over and measure for the bun feet. In this case a block was needed under the bun feet to raise the cabinet to the right height. Blocks were placed under each foot, and pilot holes were drilled into the cabinet (photo E). Then screws were set into the blocks from the inside of the cabinet. The feet themselves were threaded onto the blocks so they could be turned to raise the cabinet if needed for leveling.

8 To support the base, build a box to bring it up to the height of the other cabinets and screw through the bottom of the cabinet using 2-inch screws (photo F). The feet are decorative and don't support the weight of the cabinet.

9 Once the box is attached, flip the cabinet over, use a jigsaw to cut out a portion of the back panel for plumbing, and attach it to studs in the wall.

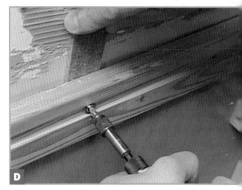
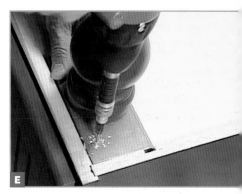

◀ INSTALLING THE VENT HOOD ▶

Mom chose a powerful 700-CFM ventilation unit, which will handily remove all cooking odors and steam from the kitchen. The unit will be housed in soffit and cowling pieces supplied by the cabinet manufacturer. First the soffit (the section that rises to the ceiling) and cowling (the section that flares out at the bottom) must be attached to the wall, and then the ventilation unit is installed inside.

You Will Need

- Pry bar
- Tape measure
- Pencil
- Level
- Screwdriver
- Aluminum duct tape
- Tin snips
- Sheet metal screws
- 2" deck screws

1 Find the center point on the wall and mark it with a pencil. Then mark the center point on the back of the soffit (photo A).

2 You want the hood to be centered over the stove, so measure and mark the center of the stove opening on the wall. Using a level, transfer that line up the wall.

3 Raise the soffit to the ceiling and make sure the center lines match up. Secure the soffit to the wall using one 2-inch deck screw (photo B). Check for level, then add the rest of the screws. Make sure the screws go into wall studs.

4 Lift the cowling up to the soffit and join the two pieces together with more deck screws.

5 Connect elbow pieces with aluminum duct tape and attach them to the vent (photo C). Put it in place inside the soffit leading to the existing vent piping in the wall.

6 Cut the vent pipe with tin snips and secure it with sheet metal screws. Run aluminum duct tape around the connection.

7 Attach the mounting bracket to the cowling. Later, you'll screw the vent unit into this piece.

8 Screw the bottom piece of the vent liner into place at the bottom of the cowling using screws supplied with the vent unit (photo D).

9 Lift the vent unit into place (photo E). Screw the unit into the mounting bracket up top, and then screw the bottom piece of the vent liner into the vent unit.

10 Attach the faceplates to the vent. Once the hood is completely installed, consider hiring a professional electrician to make the final hookups.

A

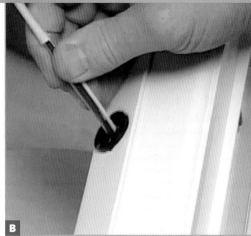

B

▰ INSTALLING UNDER-COUNTER LIGHTS ▰

To give Mom some additional task lighting, under-cabinet lights were installed. It's a simple project—just connect the hot, neutral, and ground wires to the hot, neutral, and ground wires coming out of the wall. In this case, my brother, a licensed electrician, had already brought the wires to a spot right under the upper cabinets to feed into the light units.

You Will Need

▰ Under-counter fixtures

▰ Wire stripper

▰ Screwdriver and screws

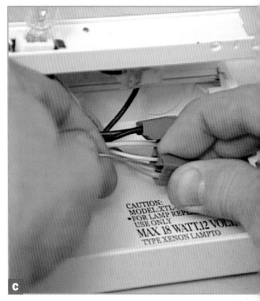

C

1 Snap the press-on fitting into its place on the light box (photo A). This fitting captures the wiring that enters the fixture.

2 Make sure the main power is off. Then strip back the outer insulation on the wire coming out of the wall with a wire stripper, exposing the hot, neutral, and ground wires.

3 Feed the wires into the fixture through the fitting (photo B). Make sure the outer insulation enters the box.

4 Strip ½-inch of insulation off the individual feed wires in the fixture box.

5 Slide the stripped wires into the corresponding wire connector boxes that come with the lighting fixture (photo C). White to white (neutral), black to black (hot), and bare to green (ground).

6 Push the excess wire into the wall, then hang the light on the bottom of the cabinet with screws (photo D). Snap in the opaque glass panel.

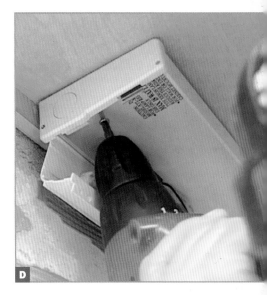

D

PERFORATED BACKSPLASH

Before installing a perforated backsplash made of 18-gauge stainless steel over the range area, we placed a piece of beadboard skin over the wall. That way, if someone looks through the perforated metal, they'll see something that matches the surrounding cabinetry.

You Will Need

- Safety glasses
- Precut backsplash
- Beadboard
- Circular saw
- Tape measure
- Construction adhesive
- Caulk gun
- Drill
- 1¼" deck screws
- Pencil

1 Cut the beadboard to size and mark the wall (photo A, above top).

2 Apply a bead of construction adhesive to the back of the beadboard, place the board on the wall, and attach it with 1¼-inch deck screws (photo B, middle).

3 Raise the perforated panel to the wall and secure it to the studs with 1¼-inch deck screws (photo C, right).

BUILT-IN MICROWAVE

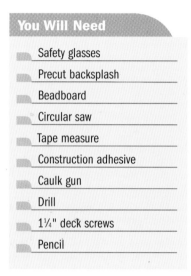

Mom ordered a cabinet specifically for a microwave. It came with wide trim around the edges so that the smallest microwave could slide right in. Since this microwave is larger, some of the frame had to be cut away.

You Will Need

- Painter's tape
- Jigsaw
- Trim

1 Mark cuts for the microwave on the standard microwave frame. Tape the surface of the frame and the shoe of the jigsaw so you don't damage the cabinet finish. Cut with a jigsaw (photo A, top left).

2 Place the microwave in the cabinet. Finish with trim to hold the microwave in place and cover the edges of the frame (photo B, below left).

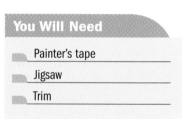

You Will Need

- Reciprocating saw
- Acetone
- Painter's tape
- Utility knife
- Carpenter's square
- Wood shims
- Razorblade
- 5-minute epoxy
- Cloth
- Silicone
- Level
- Silicone

SINK AND COUNTERTOPS

These natural stone countertops are honed slate from Vermont. After the slate was quarried, it was cut into 1½-inch slabs and then fabricated into a countertop. But before the counters could be attached to the cabinets, the under-mount sink had to be installed.

1 Use the countertop as a template and mark where you need to cut the cabinets for the sink (photo A).

2 Remove the counter and cut out the excess lumber with a reciprocating saw on both sides of the sink cutout (photo B).

3 Put the countertop facedown on a steady work surface. With a cloth dipped in acetone, wipe down the countertop where the sink will touch it so the silicone will stick to the surface. Slide the sink into place and trace the outline with a pencil (photo C).

4 Remove the sink and run a bead of silicone inside the mark. Set the sink back into place.

5 This counter was already drilled and anchored, so the sink clips were simply screwed into place (photo D). Once the sink is secure, flip the counter back over onto the base cabinets.

6 Set the remaining countertop pieces and make sure they're level. Since these are so heavy, it's easier to secure them with silicone from underneath. Slide out the drawers, reach under the cabinet, and run a bead of silicone around the edge of the cabinet and the countertops.

7 To seal the seams between countertop pieces, first protect the surface with painter's tape. Run a piece of tape over the seam and use a utility knife to carefully score the tape.

8 Use a carpenter square to make two to three reference marks across both sides of the tape, and then pull the counters about ¾ inch apart.

9 With a wood shim, butter the inside of the countertop seam with epoxy (photo E). Push the countertop back into place, making sure you line up the reference marks. Drag a razorblade over the tape to work epoxy into the seams and make sure there are no air pockets. Peel off the tape once the epoxy is dry.

A

B

C

D

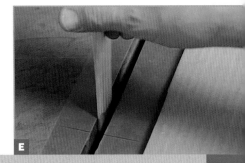

E

diy
.network

COUNTRY COTTAGE

About the only thing going for this dark and dreary 1960s kitchen was its size. The homeowners wanted to put the remodel on the back burner for a while, but just six months after they moved into the house, the project moved up to number one on their list.

BEFORE: Anybody in there? The homeowners hated having to peer under those massive upper cabinets.

AFTER: You'd never guess this bright and sunny space is the same kitchen.

◢ PROJECT SUMMARY ◣

The existing cabinet boxes were in good shape, so to save money the homeowners simply bought new door and drawer faces and gave everything a fresh coat of paint. The bank of upper cabinets obstructing the view from the kitchen to the eating area was removed, which really opened up the space. The homeowners installed beadboard on all the walls, both as wainscot and backsplash, which complements the new butcher-block countertop. A golden hardwood floor was installed right over the old vinyl. The look was completed with new light fixtures, a fireclay sink, new matching appliances, and charming touches like the blackboard message door.

TOP RIGHT: The fireclay sink, period-designed faucet, and brushed nickel cabinet pulls work well together. **RIGHT:** A door leading to the basement blends in with the rest of the kitchen after being faced with wainscot and blackboard paint. **ABOVE:** Without that bank of low cabinets, there's a clear view from the kitchen to the eating area.

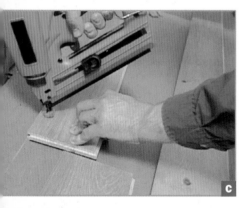

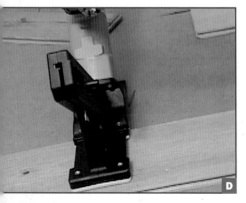

◢◤ INSTALLING A HARDWOOD PINE FLOOR ◢◤

The homeowners chose prefinished hardwood pine plank flooring. Luckily, their existing vinyl floor was smooth and in good condition, so they were able to install the hardwood floor right over it. The existing vinyl acts as a vapor barrier, so they needed only to cover it with a layer of rosin paper to keep the floor from squeaking.

You Will Need

Safety glasses	Tape measure
Broom	Chalk line
Shop vacuum	Chop or miter saw
Rosin paper	Impulse finish nailer
Utility knife	1¾" galvanized finish nails
Hammer tacker and staples	Pneumatic flooring nailer
Wood putty	Air compressor
Knee pads	

1 Lay down the rosin paper by rolling it out and overlapping each piece by at least 6 inches. Tack it into place with a hammer tacker (photo A).

2 Make sure the first row of plank flooring is straight, as you'll build on this line to finish the rest of the floor. To do this, find the longest wall in the room and make marks on the floor at an equal distance on each end of the wall. Then snap a chalk line through the marks so you have a straight line equidistant along the wall. Double-check your line by measuring from it to the other side of the room to see whether it's straight. Then adjust the first line if necessary; you may have to compromise based on how square the room is.

3 Choose the longest pieces of wood floor planks and lay them in one row along the chalk line (photo B). Make sure the ends of the boards are tight and flush against each other. Otherwise, slanting will occur and get worse as you go along.

4 Face-nail the boards using an impulse nailer with 1¾-inch galvanized finish nails (photo C). Set the nailer to sink the nails just below the surface. You will hide these holes later with wood putty. Sink one nail every 6 to 8 inches.

5 Cut the boards to length as you go, using a chop saw or miter saw. Blind-nail the tongues of the planks to the floor as you lay them, using a manual or pneumatic flooring nailer (photo D).

You Will Need

- Safety glasses
- Pencil
- Tape measure
- 6' level
- Speed square
- Japanese pull saw
- Reciprocating saw
- Hammer
- Small pry bar

A

◢ MODIFYING EXISTING CABINETS ▶

The homeowners wanted to slide their range over about a foot so it would not be so close to the door. To do this, they had to remove a small section of the cabinets.

1 With the old countertop removed, use a Japanese pull saw to cut through the top stile of the base cabinet (photo A).

2 Use a reciprocating saw to cut through the back and bottom of the frame (photo B).

3 Once the frame is cut, use a prybar to remove the pieces (photo C).

B

TIPS | DIY Network Home Improvement

HIDING THE DAMAGE

With wood stained cabinets, it takes some artistry to hide the damage done by cutting away a section. But if you plan to paint the cabinets, the damage will be easily hidden.

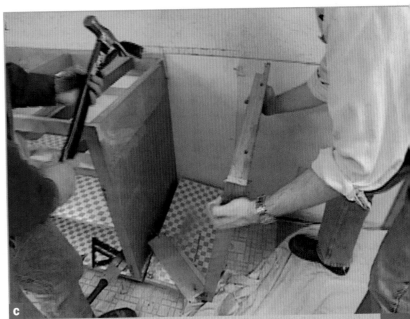

C

◄ INSTALLING BEADBOARD ►

4 x 8 sheets of beadboard were used to cover the back of one row of cabinets facing the dining area, as well as the walls above the countertops and around the room. To start, the homeowners removed the laminate sheets from the backsplash area. Then they shut off the power and removed the receptacle covers. Remove any window trim if the beadboard will go up to the edge of the window.

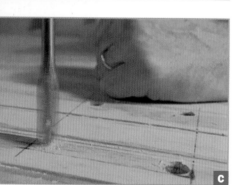

You Will Need

Safety glasses	Framing square
Pencil	Paneling adhesive
Gloves	Caulk gun
Tape measure	Jigsaw
Small pry bar	2' level
Screwdriver	Spade bit
¼" beadboard sheets	Impulse finish nailer
Cordless drill	1¼" nails
Circular saw	Stud finder

1 Measure and cut the panels of beadboard using a circular saw. Use a circular saw with a cutting guide and attached vacuum to gather sawdust (photo A).

2 Run a ¼-inch bead of adhesive all over the back of the panel, keeping about 1 inch away from the edge. Then press the panel into place. Drive nails through the panels, making sure they hit solid wood (photo B) or a stud in the wall.

3 If you need to place the beadboard around obstacles, such as electrical receptacles and switches, the trick is to make accurate measurements from the nearest wall to each side of the obstacle. Then transfer the measurements to the beadboard and make your marks. Use a spade bit to drill pilot holes at each corner (photo C).

4 Placing the jigsaw blade into a pilot hole, cut out each section (photo D).

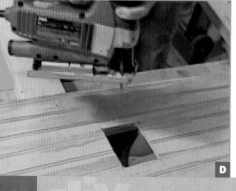

You Will Need

Screwdriver	Hole saw
Hammer	Router
Beadboard	Rabbet bit
1x trim	2' level
Safety glasses	Impulse finish nailer
Pencil	1¼" nails
Chop saw	Painter's tape
Circular saw	Chalkboard paint
Wood glue	Brush

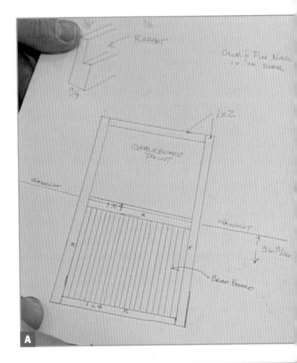

A

MAKING A MESSAGE CENTER

The door to the basement lacked the charm of the new kitchen, so the homeowners thought of an inexpensive way to spruce it up. The same type of beadboard was used to cover the bottom portion of the door, and the top was painted with chalkboard paint so it can be used to jot down messages.

1 Start by making a diagram of the project (photo A) that shows the dimensions of the door, beadboard section, and trim pieces. Remove the door from its hinges and take off the old doorknob. Using a level, mark a line across the bottom half of the door at the same height as the wainscot around the room.

2 Use a circular saw to cut the beadboard and lay it over the bottom portion of the door. Measure and cut trim pieces to go around it, and then use a router to cut a rabbet joint around the edge of the trim pieces that surround the beadboard (photo B) so that they lie smoothly over the edge.

3 Use wood glue and nails to attach the beadboard and trim pieces (photo C). Then cover the top of the door with blackboard paint, following the instructions on the can.

4 Use a hole saw to make a new hole for the doorknob. Put the door back on its hinges and reinstall the doorknob.

B

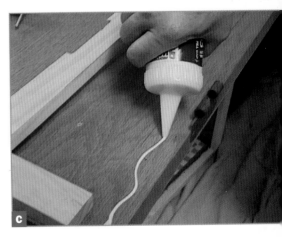

C

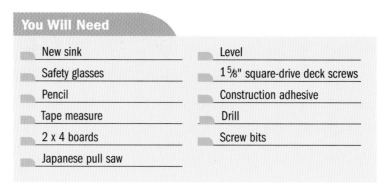

You Will Need

New sink		Level	
Safety glasses		1⅝" square-drive deck screws	
Pencil		Construction adhesive	
Tape measure		Drill	
2 x 4 boards		Screw bits	
Japanese pull saw			

DRY-FITTING THE SINK

This fireclay sink was handmade in England and fired at more than 2,000 degrees, making it similar to a fine piece of pottery. Because the sink is so heavy and would be mounted underneath the countertop, the homeowners needed to add some 2 x 4 support brackets for it to sit on.

1 Measure the height of the sink and then transfer that measurement to the inside of the cabinet (photo A). Make one mark toward the back wall of the cabinet and one toward the front. Using a level, draw a line to connect the two marks. The 2 x 4 supports will be attached along this line.

2 Run a bead of strong adhesive along the back of each 2 x 4 (photo B) and then screw the pieces into place from the side of the cabinet into the 2 x 4s using two 1⅝-inch square-drive deck screws for each 2 x 4. In this case, the 2 x 4s were doubled up because the sink is so heavy.

3 The front of the cabinet needs to be cut out to fit the apron-front sink. Use a Japanese pull saw to remove the front stile (photo C).

4 Slide the sink into place along the tops of the 2 x 4 braces (photo D) and check it for level.

TIPS
DIY Network
Home Improvement

FILL STOCK
When you make alterations to stock cabinets, you're often left with visible gaps. Use fill stock from the manufacturer to cover those gaps.

A

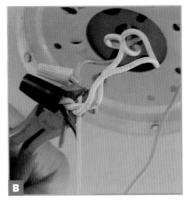

B

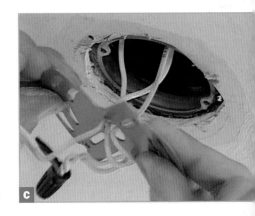

C

D

CHANGING THE LIGHT FIXTURES

Reproduction period light fixtures were chosen to go with the new style of the kitchen. Remember, before working on any electrical project, turn off power to the circuit.

You Will Need

- New light fixtures
- Ladder
- Screwdriver
- Cordless drill
- Wire cutters
- Wire nuts

1 First remove the old lighting fixtures. Unscrew the light bulbs and remove any shades or glass globes. Then unscrew the escutcheon to get at the wiring (photo A). Check again that the power is off before going any further.

2 Cut the old wires with a pair of wire cutters (photo B).

3 Unscrew the cap and remove the universal cross bar (photo C).

4 Slip the new cross bar that's included with the fixture over the existing wires and screw it into place. Then connect the wires from the new fixture to those coming out of the junction box in the ceiling with insulated wire nuts (photo D).

5 Screw the base tight to the ceiling (photo E).

6 Screw in the light bulb. Now restore electrical power to the room and test to see that everything works. If it does, screw on the cover (photo F) and the job is finished. If not, retrace your steps, and then ask an electrician to check it if you can't figure out what's wrong.

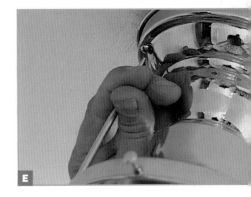

E

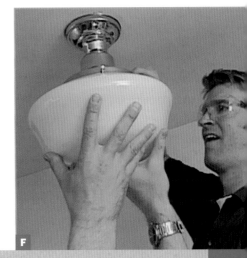

F

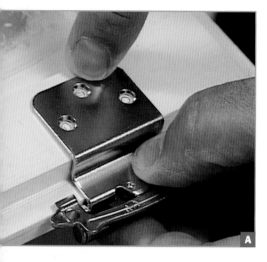

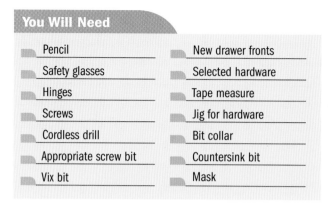

You Will Need

Pencil	New drawer fronts
Safety glasses	Selected hardware
Hinges	Tape measure
Screws	Jig for hardware
Cordless drill	Bit collar
Appropriate screw bit	Countersink bit
Vix bit	Mask

◄ INSTALLING DOORS AND DRAWER FACES ►

After priming and painting the old cabinets, new doors, and drawer faces, the homeowners were ready to put them all together. Before you order new doors and drawer faces, it's crucial to measure each existing door and drawer face. You don't want to assume that they're all the same size. Create a system for keeping track of which one will go where.

1 Attach the hinges to the doors one door at a time. Set the hinges one hinge length from the top and bottom corners of the door. Mark the holes with a pencil (photo A).

2 Remove the hinge and make pilot holes on the marks. In this case, a vix bit was used, which is self-centering and keeps the holes from being drilled too deep. Start with the center hole to make sure the hinge will align properly. Once the pilot holes are drilled, screw the hinge to the door (photo B).

3 Take the door over to the cabinet box and position it so that it will open facing the right direction. Line up the door inside the opening so it's centered from top to bottom and flush on the side with the hinges.

4 Screw in the top hinge first (photo C), then the bottom one. Use screws with the same finish as whatever hinges you've chosen.

5 Once all the doors are installed, move on to mounting the new drawer faces to the existing drawers. Cut off the old drawer face edges so the new ones will sit flush. You could take your own measurements to make sure each drawer handle is lined up, or you can use a jig to quickly find the right spots. First measure the drawer face from left to right and make a mark at the center. Line the jig up on that center mark, and it will show you where to drill the holes for the handle based on the handle size you have (photo D).

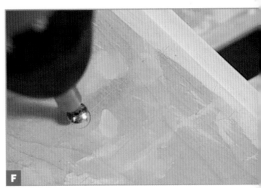

TIPS | DIY Network Home Improvement

POWER-TOOL SAFETY

Remember to always have your power tools unplugged when making adjustments, and wear safety goggles and a mask when using a power tool that generates dust.

6 Mark the holes shown on the jig with the drill bit (photo E). In this case, the hardware was so large that a countersink hole was needed. If you need to do this, use a bit collar to make sure you don't drill too deep. Screw the handles on from the inside of the drawer (photo F).

7 To attach the new fronts to the old drawers, first mark three spots on the inside of the drawer, being careful to avoid the screws for the hardware (photo G).

8 Use those marks to drill countersink holes, then pilot holes for the screws, and then drive three screws through the old door face into the new one (photo H). Be careful not to drive the screws too far.

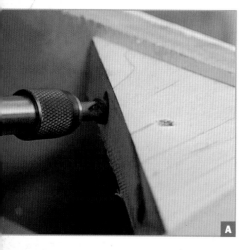

A

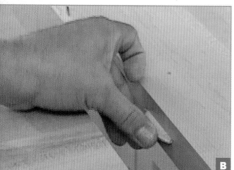

B

INSTALLING A BUTCHER-BLOCK COUNTERTOP

This butcher-block countertop is made of strips of Northern hard maple that were pressed together and then coated with an acrylic finish. Make sure the butcher-block counters arrive a few days before you need to install them. Because wood expands and contracts based on the temperature and moisture level in the room, it's best to let the wood acclimate to its new environment before screwing it into place.

You Will Need

- New countertops
- Mounting blocks
- Sawhorses
- Wood biscuits
- Miter buckles
- Screwdriver
- Deck screws

1 Mount the countertop to the cabinet bases by screwing each section to a triangular mounting block. Screw these blocks into each corner of the cabinet (photo A).

2 Each section of the counter-top needs to be attached to its neighbor to create a strong, seamless finish. Slide one section onto sawhorses for easier access, then insert a biscuit into the center of the counter (using the predrilled slot) to keep the pieces level (photo B).

3 Insert a miter buckle into a predrilled hole underneath the counter (photo C) and tighten it below the counter. The miter buckle will pull the pieces of butcher block together tightly.

4 Once the sections are joined together, slide them into place over the base cabinets.

C

A

B

You Will Need

▶	New sink	▶	2" screws
▶	New faucet	▶	Corner supports
▶	Tape measure	▶	Silicone
▶	Cordless drill	▶	Caulk gun
▶	Forstner bit		

C

◢ INSTALLING THE SINK AND FAUCET ◣

The butcher-block counter had an existing cutout for the sink but not ones for the main faucet and separate drinking water faucet. Before cutting holes in the counter, the homeowners removed the sink so as not to damage it.

1 Decide where you want the kitchen faucet and accessories such as a sink sprayer or drinking water faucet to be, and mark those spots on the countertop (photo A).

2 Use a drill equipped with a forstner bit to cut out the holes (photo B), which in this case includes three holes for the separate hot and cold water lines and the drinking water line.

3 Slide the sink back into place. Lift the butcher-block counter around it and run a bead of silicone under the edges (photo C). Press the counter down and the sink will be secure. Hire a plumber to make the final faucet connections.

4 Now you can screw the corner supports to the butcher block from underneath (photo D).

D

48-HOUR TUSCAN

These homeowners fell in love with the Tuscan region while on their honeymoon in Italy. So when it came time to give their kitchen a face-lift, they chose colors and textures that would remind them of their time in Tuscany. In just 48 hours, and with a little help, they transformed their average kitchen into a warm and sunny slice of Italy.

◢ PROJECT SUMMARY ◣

A decorative painter helped the homeowners come up with a faux-finish treatment for the walls and cabinets. Professionals installed new limestone countertops, a range, and a built-in microwave. Luckily the floor had been updated recently and worked with the new color scheme. A freestanding island that separated the kitchen from the eating area was spruced up with paint and new hardware, put in the center of the kitchen, and outfitted with a limestone countertop, effectively doubling the amount of counter space in the kitchen. New backsplash tiles went up quickly, as did the homemade panels that now cover the refrigerator and dishwasher.

AFTER: Warm colors, a tiled backsplash, and upgraded appliances made all the difference in this kitchen.

BEFORE: This functional kitchen needed a little flair.

You Will Need

- Bucket
- Joint compound mix
- 4" putty knife
- Drop cloths
- Drill with a mixing bit
- Painter's tape
- Paint tray and liners
- Rollers
- Brushes
- Primer
- Paint
- Paint conditioner

TEXTURING AND PAINTING THE WALLS

The homeowners first textured their walls by skim-coating them with joint compound, and then covered the walls with three colors of paint. The result is a rough, old-world surface with warm color that matches the Tuscan style they were going for.

1 Prepare the area by putting down drop cloths and taping off any walls and cabinets you don't want to texture and paint.

2 Mix the lightweight joint compound in the bucket according to the instructions on the bag. Apply small amounts to the wall in a random pattern using a 4-inch putty knife (photo A). Spread a thin layer in even passes with smooth, steady strokes.

Continue over the entire wall, overlapping strokes slightly (it's not necessary to cover every inch of the wall; some bare spots are fine). Let the joint compound dry before painting it.

3 When you're ready to paint, pour equal amounts of primer and base paint into a roller tray and stir with a brush (photo B). You can't just go straight to the first coat of paint because

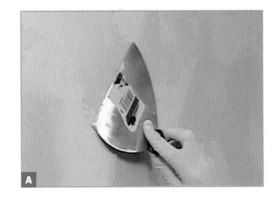

A

B

joint compound needs to be primed to seal the texture in place. Tinting the primer with the base coat color will help you avoid having to do a second coat of base color. Be sure to keep the ratio of primer and paint the same for subsequent batches.

4 Use a brush to cut in the paint near the ceiling and corners. Then use a roller to coat the entire wall (photo C). Let this coat dry before moving on to the next step.

5 Mix the second color, in this case a burnt umber, with paint conditioner using a 50:50 ratio. Paint conditioner keeps the paint fluid, reduces visible brush marks, and dilutes the color, making it more like a glaze that can move around on the wall longer before it dries. Working in small sections,

lightly brush this coat onto the wall in swirling motions (photo D), making sure to get the paint into all the crevices.

6 Quickly wipe off the excess with a dry rag (photo E). Don't worry about wiping it out of every crack and crevice—those darker areas will emphasize the wall's texture. Follow steps 5 and 6 across the entire wall.

7 Once all the umber color is on and has dried, apply a third highlight color using a dry-brush technique. Dip a dry brush into the highlight paint and wipe the bristles on a sheet of newspaper until most of the paint has come off. Then use quick strokes in random passes to apply the color to the wall (photo F).

You Will Need

Drill	Tape measure
Screwdriver bits	Paint
Orbital palm sander	Primer
Tack cloth	Paintbrush
Disposable gloves	Paint conditioner
Hot glue gun	Newspaper
Glue sticks	Cotton rags
Decorative wood pieces	New glass knobs

A

PAINTING THE CABINETS

The existing cabinets were in good condition, so the home-owners simply gave them a new coat of paint using the same faux technique they used on the walls. They also added relief pieces on the doors to give them a decorative flourish.

1 Remove the doors from their hinges, making sure to mark each one so you know where it belongs. Remove all the hardware and save the hinges and screws.

2 Create a workspace outside where you can lay out all the doors. Using an orbital palm sander, sand the front of the doors to remove the existing finish (photo A). Wipe off the doors with a tack cloth.

B

3 The homeowners chose laminated wood relief pieces (photo B) to add some Tuscan style to their flat-panel doors. Decide where you want the decorative pieces to go and measure and mark each door so that the pieces are consistently placed from one door to the next.

4 Use a hot glue gun to attach the pieces to the doors. Wear gloves as the glue is extremely hot, and move quickly because the glue dries fast.

5 Once the decorative pieces are set, it's time to faux paint the cabinet doors. Mix the primer and some of the base-coat color in a 50:50 ratio and brush it on to cover the surface (photo C). Let it dry.

C

6 Then brush on an undiluted layer of the base-coat color, following the grain of the wood (photo D). Let it dry.

D

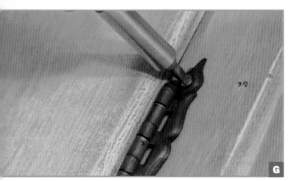

7 Mix the second color of paint, in this case a burnt umber, with a latex paint conditioner, again using a 50:50 ratio. The conditioner gives the paint a glaze effect, reduces visible brushstrokes, and dilutes the color. Apply this layer using a dry-brush technique. To do this, dip a dry paintbrush into the mixture of paint and conditioner and then wipe the bristles a few times on a piece of newspaper until the brush is mostly dry. Then quickly brush over the surface of the door, which will leave a small amount of color behind. Be sure to get into all the crevices of the decorative pieces, then wipe the door with a dry rag while the paint is still wet (photo E). Leave some paint in the grooves of the decorative pieces. Let this layer dry.

8 A final highlight color is dry-brushed on with gold paint (photo F). Again, dip the brush into the paint and wipe the excess onto a piece of newspaper before applying the paint to the door. Use quick strokes.

9 The cabinet boxes were painted with the same technique. Once everything is dry, the doors can be reinstalled.

10 Put on new knobs using the existing holes. Reattach the old hinges to the doors using the old screws and existing holes, then attach the doors to the cabinet boxes (photo G). Have one person hold up the door and another person screw the hinges into place with a cordless drill.

PANEL KITS FOR APPLIANCES

The homeowners found a company that sells custom panel kits to use on existing appliances. They painted the panels using the same technique they used on the cabinet doors. Then they attached the frames to the front of the refrigerator and dishwasher, giving the old appliances a built-in look.

You Will Need

- Drop cloth or paper
- Painter's tape
- V-notched trowel
- Tile
- Wet saw
- Premixed mastic
- Bucket of water
- Bag of grout
- Drill with paddle mixer
- Rubber grout float
- Sponge and rags

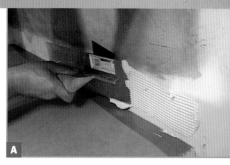
A

◢ TILING THE BACKSPLASH ◣

The backsplash tile that the homeowners chose looks a lot like the limestone countertops, but it's actually made of porcelain.

1 Prep the area by covering the countertop with a drop cloth or paper. Tape off the back edge of the countertop.

2 Lay out the tiles to see how they will fit, then make adjustments to ensure you have the most whole tiles possible.

3 Using a V-notched trowel tipped at a 30-degree angle, apply mastic to the bottom area of the backsplash (photo A).

4 Press each section of tiles into place (photo B). Because these tiles are on a mesh backing, no spacers are required.

5 Put up the border tile by back-buttering each piece—applying a small amount of mastic directly onto the back of the tile (photo C) before setting it into place. Allow the mastic to dry before grouting.

6 Tape above and around the edges of the tile so you don't get grout on the freshly painted walls. Mix the grout according to the directions on the package. Using a rubber grout float at a 30-degree angle, push the grout into the spaces between the tiles (photo D).

7 Wipe the grout off with a damp sponge, rinsing after each pass in a bucket of clean water. Wipe until the tiles are clean and the grout lines are even (photo E).

B

C

D

TIPS
DIY Network Home Improvement

ORDER OF WORK
Start at the bottom and work your way up, as the weight of the tiles can cause them to slide down the wall. Wipe off excess mastic from the front of the tiles as you go.

E

TIMELESS TRADITIONAL

The kitchen of this 1918 bungalow was last remodeled in the 1970s, and time had definitely passed it by. The existing layout was odd, with the refrigerator far outside the work triangle in the seating area and the cooktop under the window. With a brick backsplash, worn vinyl flooring in a loud pattern, glass block window, and cabinets too far gone to salvage, this kitchen needed to be completely ripped out and put back together.

BEFORE: With a black range sitting under the window where the sink should be, the refrigerator in the seating area, and the overall style of the space, this kitchen needed a major reconfiguration.

AFTER: Now the sink is under the new window, the refrigerator is in the work triangle, and the space functions much more efficiently. The bright colors and modern concrete and steel amenities match the style of the current homeowners. A built-in banquette seating area in the breakfast nook ties in with the kitchen cabinets.

◢◣ **PROJECT SUMMARY** ◢◣

The homeowners hired a kitchen designer who is also an architect to come up with a new plan. She fixed the work triangle problems by bringing the refrigerator back into the main work area, moving the sink under the window, and making a spot for a range across from the refrigerator. The adjoining living room was also part of this remodel, so new hardwood floors would be installed in both rooms to visually connect them. Once the owners finished the demolition, which included ripping the walls down to the studs, removing existing vinyl and carpet, and replacing the glass block window, they installed an in-floor radiant heat system, Brazilian cherry hardwood floors, new cabinets, and a concrete countertop. After they added some bright paint, a tile backsplash that connects the dark countertop to the light cabinets, new appliances, and banquette seating in the breakfast nook, the new kitchen couldn't have looked any less like the old.

Sleek frameless cabinets look great with the concrete countertops and stone backsplash. A downdraft vent behind the range means there's no need for a vent hood blocking the view to the family room. It pops up only when in use.

A

B

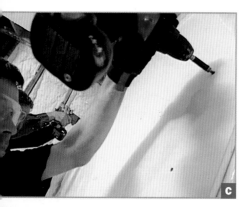

C

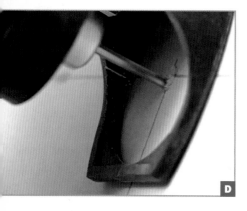

D

You Will Need

Dust mask and gloves	Drill
Safety glasses	Rotary cutting tool
Precut insulation	Spiral bit
4-mill polyethylene sheeting	Self-adhesive fiberglass tape
Utility knife	Joint compound
Hammer tacker	8" taping knife
Staples	Drywall sandpaper sheets
Tape measure	Plastic Sheeting
Framing square	Painter's tape
½" drywall and 1⅝" screws	

PUTTING THE WALLS BACK TOGETHER

Because this kitchen had a variety of finishes on the walls (including a brick backsplash, some drywall, and some lath and plaster) the easiest thing to do was to remove it all and start from scratch. Removing drywall and lath and plaster is a messy job, but it's as simple as ripping the materials off the studs with gloved hands. Always work carefully around walls with wires or pipes inside. Once you're down to the studs, complete any electrical or plumbing work that's easier done with the walls open. When you're ready to close them up, check to see what the R-value requirement for insulation is in your city, and then buy precut pieces of insulation to stuff between the studs of all exterior walls.

1 Put on heavy gloves and a dust mask. Fill the spaces between the studs with precut, unfaced insulation (photo A).

2 Cover insulation with 4-mil polyethylene sheeting to create a vapor barrier. Staple the sheeting into place with a tack hammer (photo B). Cut out around any window and door openings with a utility knife. For more information about removing interior walls made of drywall or lath and plaster, see pages 159-160 in chapter 3.

3 Once the insulation is in place, it's time to put up the new drywall. Run pieces of 4 x 8 drywall either horizontally or vertically across the wall—whichever way results in the fewest seams. Screw the pieces to the studs every 16 inches using 1⅝-inch drywall screws (photo C).

4 If you measure and mark all electrical boxes and windows, you can place a large sheet of drywall over the entire area and then come back with a rotary cutting tool (photo D) and cut out the marked areas.

5 Run self-adhesive fiberglass tape over the seams between the sheets of drywall (photo E).

6 Apply a liberal coat of joint compound over the fiberglass tape using an 8-inch taping knife. While the compound is still wet, make a smooth pass over the area with the taping knife to remove excess material and leave as smooth a finish as possible (photo F).

7 Once the joint compound has dried, sand the edges smooth. This makes quite a mess, so put up some plastic sheeting over the doorways and any vents. Otherwise, the dust will travel throughout the house.

RADIANT HEAT SYSTEM

The family room adjoining this kitchen was an addition, and it gets cold and drafty in winter. So the homeowners took the opportunity to add an in-floor heat system as a supplement to their forced-air heat system before the new floors were installed. They chose a low-profile electric radiant heat strip system that can go under any type of flooring. It works by sending 24 volts of power through wires on each side of the strip, heating them up. In turn, heat is transferred through the wood floor and into the room. A professional installed this system, but if you decide to do it yourself, be sure to first make a drawing of your space to determine how many strips of thermoplastic polymer you will need to cut. The strips are rolled out across the subfloor, cut into sections with scissors, and stapled down. Then the terminal wires are connected. Follow the instructions that come with the system you choose. You will likely need to call an electrician to make the final hookups and install a switch. See pages 143-144 for more information.

You Will Need

- Safety glasses
- Gloves
- Pry bar
- Tape measure
- 4 x 8 sheets of ⅝" plywood
- Spade bit
- Jigsaw
- Table saw
- Rapid-load screw gun
- Galvanized nails
- Rosin paper
- Hammer tacker
- Impulse nailer

◀ INSTALLING THE SUBFLOOR ▶

Once the old vinyl and carpet were removed, the homeowners were left with an uneven subfloor, so they needed to put down a new layer of plywood to create a stable surface for their hardwood flooring. When the homeowners took out the refrigerator, they discovered that the subfloor underneath had been damaged by a water leak. Before the new subfloor could be installed, the damaged portion had to be repaired. The damaged piece was cut out and new pieces of ⅝-inch plywood were cut to fit into the holes. They were then fastened with the same methods described below.

1 Measure the area to be covered. You will want to use as many whole sheets of 4 x 8 plywood as possible. Remember to leave a ¼-inch gap around the perimeter of the room and between sheets to allow for expansion and contraction.

2 Drive nails or screws approximately every 6 inches around the perimeter and across each piece of plywood (photo A).

3 Mark and cut out vent holes and other obstacles using a spade bit and a jigsaw. Make long cuts on the table saw.

4 Lay sheets of rosin paper over the plywood subfloor to help reduce floor squeaks. Staple them into place with a hammer tacker (photo B).

TIPS | DIY Network Home Improvement

WHY PLYWOOD?
Plywood is best for subfloors because it holds nails and screws securely. Make sure the fasteners are galvanized to prevent rusting.

You Will Need

Prefinished hardwood	Pencil
Safety glasses	Pin nailer
Knee pads	Pneumatic nailer
Gloves	Spline
Rosin paper	2" staples
Hammer tacker	Air compressor
Chalk line	Rubber mallet
Tape measure	Compound miter saw

A

◢ INSTALLING THE HARDWOOD FLOOR ◣

Brazilian cherry hardwood floors were installed in the kitchen and adjoining family room.

1 The hardest part of laying a wood floor is making sure it's square. Do this by finding the longest uninterrupted run in the room. In this case, the new floor would meet up with an existing hardwood floor, so the homeowners lined a new board up to that and measured out from the nearest wall to the far side of the strip. Mark that line with a pencil (photo A).

B

2 Now transfer that mark to the other side of the room, again with a pencil on the rosin paper. Then snap a chalk line that connects the marks across the room (photo B).

3 Lay a long piece of hardwood flooring along this line and nail it into the subfloor using a pin nailer. Then extend the line with other pieces of flooring and nail them down so you have one row that reaches across the room (photo C).

C

4 Insert a spline into the groove side of the boards (photo D) so that you can install the tongue-and-groove boards from either side of your main line. Tap the spline into place with a rubber mallet and then nail it to the board using a pin nailer.

D

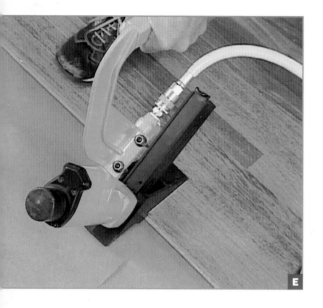

E

5 Lay boards from both sides of the main line across the room, leaving a ¼-inch gap at all the walls. When you put a piece into place, tap it with a rubber mallet to make sure it's flush.

6 Once each piece is in place, fasten to the subfloor with a pneumatic nailer equipped with 2-inch staples (photo E). Use a compound miter saw to make simple cuts. Change the blade when the saw begins to labor during a cut.

7 Cover the entire floor except for the area that the cabinets will cover. Do put the floor under the appliances so they are easier to move and replace down the line. Measure and mark how far out the cabinets will come from the wall and install one piece of hardwood strip flooring past this line to ensure that the front toekick will rest on the finished floor.

8 If you need to transition from the new floor to an existing flooring or carpet that may be at a slightly different height (usually in a doorway), buy a transition piece (photo F). Simply cut it to length and nail it into place.

TIPS
DIY Network
Home Improvement

SPECIAL SITUATIONS

In this project, a few special situations came up, such as nailing around the in-floor heating system and making a curve around the brick hearth. The homeowners brought in an expert to give them some tips. To work around the in-floor radiant heat system, they used a dado blade to cut away some of the thickness of the boards, allowing the wiring to pass underneath. To make the curved edge, they marked the pieces and used a band saw to make the cuts. Strips of cork were placed between the brick hearth and the wood floor to allow for expansion and contraction.

F

A

B

C

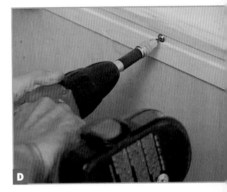

D

E

F

◢ INSTALLING CABINETS ◣

The homeowners chose semi-custom cabinets and made sure they arrived in time to keep the project moving. In this case they installed the upper cabinets first so they didn't have to reach over the lower cabinets. We used a special cabinet lift to hoist the upper cabinets into place. That way, no one would be straining to hold them up while another person worked on fastening them to the walls.

You Will Need

Cabinets	Stud finder
Cabinet lift	2" screws
Drill	Nail gun
Level	Fill stock
Ruler	

1 Draw a line to mark where the bottom of the upper cabinets will be (photo A). Then mark all the studs so you know where to set the screws.

2 Use a cabinet lift to raise the top cabinets into place (photo B). You can rent one at most tool rental centers for a reasonable day rate.

3 Make sure the cabinets are level front to back and side to side.

4 Attach the units to the walls using 2-inch screws, making sure you hit the studs (photo C). Continue until all the upper cabinets are in place.

5 Measure the first base cabinet and make a mark on the wall to indicate where the edge will go. Move the cabinet into place and check it for level, both front to back and side to side. If the floor isn't level, install the first cabinet at the highest point and shim up the rest as you go.

6 Once you're sure the unit is level, screw it into the wall, making sure you hit the studs (photo D).

7 Before installing the next two cabinets, screw their face frames together (photo E). Then slide them both into place at once and screw them into the studs.

8 Use pieces of fill stock to hide any gaps between cabinets (photo F).

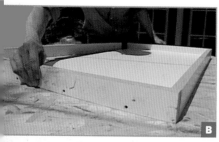

You Will Need

Luan	Drill	Goggles
Utility knife	Steel mesh	Beeswax
Straightedge	Magnesium float	Nail gun
Hot glue gun	Edger tool	Board
Table saw with guide	Steel trowel	Tape
Wheelbarrow	Foam brush	Soft cloth
Shovel	Sealer	Scraper
Palm sander	Black & white silicone	Concrete mix and pigment
Melamine	Mask	

CONCRETE COUNTERTOPS

Concrete countertops have become quite popular in kitchens because of their durability and natural look. They can be cast in place or prefabricated off site. While you can make your own concrete countertops, if your project involves a couple of turns and requires cutouts for a sink and faucet, you're likely to get a better result if you hire a professional to make them. In this case, the homeowners had the majority of their countertops prefabricated by a professional. But there was one small rectangular area that they decided to tackle on their own. Note: It takes a full 28 days for concrete countertops to cure, although it's possible to install them after about 14 days.

1 Make a template of the counter using ¼-inch sheets of luan (photo A). Once you get the right shape, trim the luan with a utility knife and a straightedge. Glue the pieces together with hot glue and write notes on the template to indicate the walls and finished edges.

TIPS | DIY Network Home Improvement

2 Use the luan template to measure and cut a form that you will pour the concrete into. Cut the form out of a piece of ¾-inch melamine and screw the four sides to the base piece (photo B). Melamine is coated with plastic resin, and its smooth surface will release the concrete easily. For this project the homeowners laid steel mesh into the form to add strength to the concrete.

TYPE OF CONCRETE
Buy concrete sold specifically for countertops and follow the manufacturer's instructions for mixing and curing.

3 Pour a bag of concrete mix into a wheelbarrow. Wear a mask, goggles, and gloves while working with the concrete.

4 You can color the concrete by either tinting it at this stage (for integral color) or applying a powdered color to the surface while the concrete is still wet (which colors just the top layer). In this case, the concrete was tinted before it was formed. Mix half a gallon of water with a pint of the liquid color, then add one gallon of water and stir (photo C).

5 When the mix is ready, shovel it into the form (photo D). Work out any large air bubbles with your gloved hands.

6 Screed the mixture by slowly pulling a board across the top (photo E). Apply even pressure on both sides of the board.

7 Press a palm sander against the edges of the form. The vibration gets rid of any air bubbles in the concrete (photo F).

8 Run a magnesium float across the top of the mold to seal the concrete to the edges and get rid of lumps (photo G).

9 Let the mold sit for 45 minutes to an hour. Once the concrete is set, run an edger tool between the mold and the concrete so you get a rounded edge, and so it comes out easily later on. Also run a steel trowel over the top to remove any surface imperfections.

10 Once the countertop has cured, remove the melamine mold, flip the countertop over (the bottom of the mold is the top of the counter) and apply a penetrating sealer to the top and sides of the countertop using a foam brush (photo H). Once the sealant is dry, after about 24 hours, coat the countertop with beeswax using a soft cloth.

11 Apply a bead of silicone to the top of each cabinet (photo I) and lower the concrete countertop pieces into place.

12 For the seams, use a small scraper to apply a gray sealant made from a mix of black and white silicone. Tape both sides of the edge so the mixture gets only in the seam (photo J).

TIPS DIY Network Home Improvement

MAINTENANCE
To maintain the countertops, simply apply beeswax every one to three months (according to how much you use your counters) and buff with a soft cloth.

F

G

H

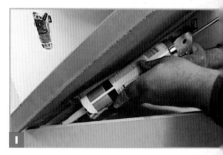

I

J

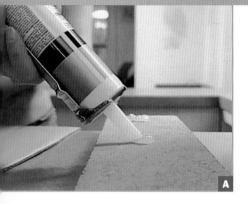

You Will Need

Concrete backsplash	Wet saw
100% silicone	Masking tape
Caulk gun	V-notch trowel
Safety glasses	Mastic
Porcelain tile	

▰ INSTALLING THE BACKSPLASH ▰

A 4-inch-tall piece of concrete provided by the countertop manufacturer acts as the immediate backsplash. But the homeowners wanted a better transition from the dark countertops to the light upper cabinets, so they installed some porcelain tile that looks like stone but is light in color. We decided to install the porcelain tiles with butt joints, meaning that each tile is pressed right up against the next and therefore no grout is needed. This isn't advisable for large areas of tiles, and especially not where tiles will get wet. Since these are placed above the concrete backsplash, it was safe to do and saved some time.

1 Apply dollops of 100 percent silicone to the middle of the concrete backsplash piece (photo A). Thick dollops will ensure better adhesion than thin lines, but be sure not to apply them too close to the edge of the concrete stone or the silicone may spill out onto the countertop. Firmly press the pieces into place (photo B).

2 To install the porcelain tiles over the concrete backsplash, first find the center of the wall to determine the starting point. Mark that spot and start with a full tile on either side of that line. Use a wet saw to make cuts (photo C) where you meet a corner or to cut around receptacles and other obstacles.

3 Before placing the tiles, lay a piece of masking tape along the edge of the backsplash to protect the concrete surface. Apply mastic adhesion to the walls evenly at a 45-degree angle using a V-notch trowel.

4 Press the tiles into the adhesive, wiggling them to set them into place (photo D).

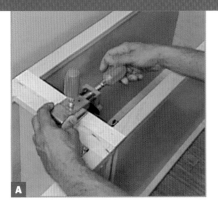

A

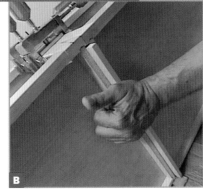

B

C

◀ BUILDING A BANQUETTE ▶

The homeowners decided to add a banquette to the kitchen for some built-in seating and extra storage. They made the banquette out of two furniture drawers purchased from the same company that made their cabinets, so the finishes matched. All they needed to do was build a platform for the drawers to sit on, then add a bench on top.

You Will Need

- 2 drawers
- Bench top
- ⅜" stock
- 2 x 4s
- 2 nailer blocks
- Impulse nailer
- Cabinet clamps
- Drill
- Screws

D

E

F

1. Use 2 x 4s to construct the platform frame and nail the pieces together.

2. Clamp the two drawer units together with a cabinet clamp (photo A).

3. Use a piece of ⅜-inch stock to fill the gap between the two drawers (photo B) and drive screws to hold it in place.

4. Nail in two nailer blocks, one on each end of the platform, to fill in the dead space between where the platform ends and the wall begins (photo C). Later, you'll screw through these pieces into the wall studs (see step 6).

5. Next, secure the platform by screwing it into the studs in the wall (photo D) rather than into the floor. This way, if you ever want to move the seating, you won't have ruined the floor.

6. Place the two cabinet drawers on top of the platform and secure them to the wall by screwing into the studs (photo E).

7. Secure the top seating area of the banquette (photo F) by attaching a couple of screws from the bottom. Then insert the drawers, add pulls, and trim out the toekick area.

91

48-HOUR LOFT KITCHEN

This loft kitchen is in a home workspace and simply lacked the sleek style of its surroundings. A kitchen designer suggested refinishing the existing cabinets, installing a new countertop, and adding black appliances to give the space a whole new look. Paul and the homeowner were able to execute the designer's plan in 48 hours with a little help from a few contractors.

To update the floor, a rubber membrane tile product that simply snaps together was installed over the existing vinyl. The cabinet boxes were in good shape, so they were refaced with a brushed aluminum laminate veneer. Professionals came in to install a unique solid surface countertop made of paper that has been impregnated with resin and then pressed and baked. It was installed just like any other solid-surface countertop. Another contractor constructed one new cabinet to house several appliances, including an under-counter refrigerator-freezer, a two-drawer dishwasher, and a built-in espresso machine. The range was replaced with a sleek black cooktop. An all-in-one microwave, convection oven, and vent hood was installed above the range. Then came the finishing touches, including a fresh coat of paint on the walls, a built-in wine rack, and new mini arc lights installed on top of the wall cabinets to give the kitchen some task lighting since the ceilings in the loft are so high.

AFTER: Not only is it sleek, modern, and more functional, this kitchen now blends nicely with the loft's design.

BEFORE: White melamine cabinets, dated countertops, and basic appliances didn't fit with the look of the rest of the loft.

A

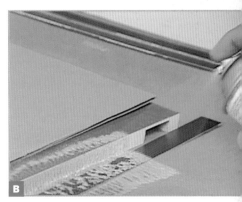

B

You Will Need

Safety glasses	80-tooth laminate blade
Pry bar	Aerosol contact cement
Drill	Painter's tape
Circular saw	Laminate roller
Level	Router with flush-cutting bit
Respirator	Dowels
Metal and black laminate	Belt sander, 80-grit sandpaper
Table saw	Tack cloth

1 Cut the metal laminate pieces to size using a table saw equipped with an 80-tooth laminate blade (photo A). Leave about half an inch of extra material around all four sides.

◀ LAMINATING THE CABINETS ▶

Instead of replacing the cabinets just because they weren't the right look for the new space, the homeowner refaced the existing doors and drawers with a metal laminate. A black laminate covers the cabinet boxes, rails, and stiles. The laminate pieces come with a film to protect them from fingerprints during installation. We started by carefully removing the kitchen cabinets. If your cabinets are sealed to the wall, you will need to use a pry bar to remove the glue or silicone. While you could laminate them in place, the process creates a lot of dust and fumes, so it's better to do it in a separate location. Be careful when removing the cabinet boxes, and mark where each box, door, and drawer goes so they can be put back easily.

2 Begin by affixing the laminate to the edges of the doors and drawer faces. Tape off the edge of the face so you don't get glue on it. Put on a respirator and make sure there's plenty of ventilation in the room. Spray both the edge of the cabinet door and the precut metal laminate strip with aerosol contact cement (photo B) and let it set up for five to 10 minutes.

3 After the cement has set, press the strip into place (photo C). Run a special laminate 3-in-1 roller over the surface to even out the glue and eliminate air bubbles.

4 Use a router to trim off the excess laminate. Hold the router flush against the edge (photo D). A flush-cutting bit with a bottom bearing ensures that you won't go any lower than the edge of the door.

5 Use a belt sander with 80-grit sandpaper to smooth the cut edges (photo E). When you're finished sanding, clean the surface with a tack cloth.

6 Now move on to the front of the doors and drawer faces. Spray the face and the laminate piece with contact glue. Once you adhere the laminate to the cabinet door, it will not move, so place four dowels on top of the door to allow you to fine tune the laminate's position before pressing it down.

7 Once you have the laminate lined up correctly, remove the dowel from the center first. Push down on the center of the laminate and then work your way out to the ends, removing one dowel at a time. Press down on the laminate as you remove each dowel (photo F). Make sure there are no bubbles.

8 Use a roller to apply pressure to the laminate and then trim the edges using the same process with the router as shown in step 5.

9 Follow the same steps to apply black laminate pieces to the cabinet boxes, including the rails, stiles, and sides (photo G).

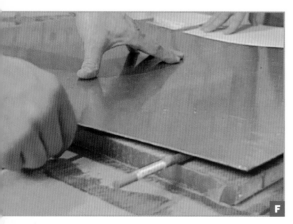

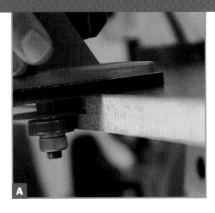

A

B

1 Make a groove in the top and bottom edges of the doors using a router with a $\frac{1}{16}$-inch dado bit with a follow bearing (photo A, top left). The bearing allows you to maintain the depth of the groove.

2 Use a compound miter saw to cut the handles to size.

3 Use a Japanese pull saw and aviation snips to cut about $\frac{1}{2}$ inch off the portion of the handle ends that fit into the groove so that they will sit flush with the edges of the door.

4 Slide each handle into the grooves and tap them into place with a rubber mallet (photo B, top right).

INSTALLING DOOR PULLS ON CABINETS

You Will Need

- Safety glasses
- Metal door handles
- Router with $\frac{1}{16}$" dado bit
- Compound miter saw
- Japanese pull saw
- Aviation snips
- Rubber mallet

Instead of standard door handles, the designer of this kitchen suggested installing pulls on the top and bottom of each door. Each door will have a groove routed in the top and bottom edge. The pulls are then tapped into place with a rubber mallet. A barbed edge on the door pulls ensures they won't fall out of place.

INSTALLING FLOOR TILES

The floor tiles are made out of recycled plastic and carpet. They come in a variety of colors, and you can install the pieces by snapping them together. This floating floor material eliminates the need for mortar and grout and can be installed over most any existing flooring.

1 Use a utility knife to cut the tabs off the edge of one row of tiles (photo A, bottom left) so they will fit flush with the edge of the carpet.

2 Lay down the tiles and interlock the opposing tabs with a rubber mallet (photo B, bottom right). Cut around obstacles with a straightedge and a utility knife.

3 Finish the edges with a coordinating T-molding.

You Will Need

- Rubber mallet
- Interlocking tiles
- Tape measure
- Utility knife
- Straightedge
- T-molding

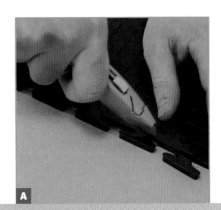

A

B

RECLAIMED CLASSIC

This 1914 house has built-in character, but it all stopped short of the kitchen. From the drop-down industrial-style ceiling to the indoor-outdoor carpet on the floor, this room needed a total renovation. With the help of a talented kitchen designer, the homeowners got a new kitchen with lots of classic charm.

BEFORE: The cabinets were in good shape, but everything else was literally falling apart.

AFTER: A fresh coat of paint brightened up the existing cabinets. The gleaming white backsplash tiles, stainless steel appliances, cabinet pulls and hinges, and a new hardwood floor make this space feel like a kitchen by the beach. Below, a built-in banquette seating area with decorative molding is a cozy spot to curl up with some coffee.

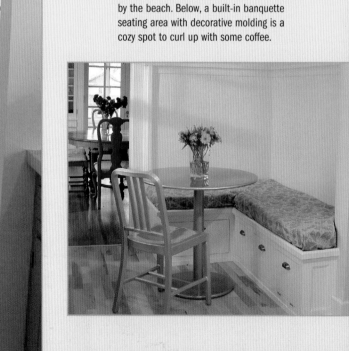

◄ PROJECT SUMMARY ►

The cabinets were in pretty good shape and could be brought back to life with new paint and hardware. The old drop-down ceiling was removed, and in its place contractors installed a solid ceiling with recessed lights. The carpet was replaced with maple hardwood flooring. A quartz countertop was installed in the kitchen, and a maple counter warmed up the breakfast nook. On the other side of the nook, there's a custom-built banquette seating area with detailed trimwork on the walls above. White ceramic subway tile covers the walls in the kitchen, and the existing windows got some new trim to match what's used elsewhere in the house. New appliances with a stainless steel, smudge-proof finish have a clean design and are perfect for a home with children. The refrigerator, which was moved from another wall in the kitchen, got a custom surround to make it look like a built-in.

LEFT: The sea green quartz countertop with deep undermount sink makes a dramatic statement.
RIGHT: A sleek refrigerator sits in a newly constructed alcove.

A

B

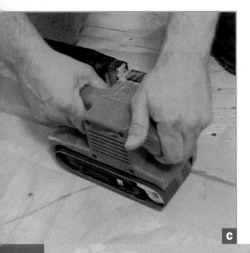

C

You Will Need

Eye protection	Belt sander
Prefinished wood flooring	Laser level
½" plywood	Tape measure
Drill	Pneumatic stapler
Tapping block	Air compressor
Screws	³/₁₆" crown staples, 1" long
Skim-coat mortar	Spline material

INSTALLING HARDWOOD FLOOR

Once the existing carpet was removed from the floor and all the cabinets were temporarily moved to another part of the house, the homeowners were ready to install their prefinished maple wood floor. They started by installing new underlayment over the subfloor. While underlayment can sometimes be stapled to the subfloor, in this case we used screws because the floor had a lot of squeaks and the screws would fix most of them.

1 Cover the floor with ½-inch plywood. Stagger the joints to ensure the least amount of flex in the subfloor.

2 Drive screws into the subfloor every 3 inches on seams and 6 inches apart throughout each piece of plywood. Start in the corner and work your way out. A standing deck gun, which can be rented, allows you to stand up and rapid-fire the screws into place (photo A).

3 Fill in all the gaps and seams that are ¼ inch or larger with skim-coat mortar (photo B).

4 Once the patching compound is dry, use a belt sander to smooth out the edges (photo C).

5 Now you're ready to install the wood floor. Use a laser level to determine a reference line as a starting point. Take two measurements, one from each end of the room, to make sure the line is an equal distance from the wall.

TIPS
DIY Network
Home Improvement

GOING THE OTHER WAY
To lay strips going the other direction from your first line, tap a spline into the groove, which provides a tongue to nail the next piece into.

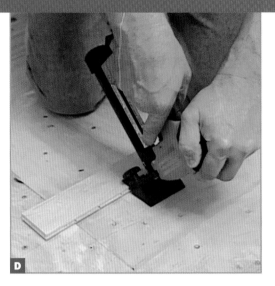

D

E

6 Line up the tongue of the first board with the reference line. Secure the board with a pneumatic stapler for hardwood floors (photo D), using 1-inch-long, ³⁄₁₆-inch crown staples every 6 to 8 inches. Make sure your staple gun is adjusted to countersink the staples so that they don't interfere with the next course of flooring.

7 Stagger the boards so that the ends are at least 6 inches apart. Use the factory-supplied tapping block to tighten boards as you go (photo E).

◀ PAINTING THE CABINETS ▶

Since the existing wood cabinets were in good shape, the homeowners decided to paint them rather than replace them. They used a pale green color on the bottom cabinets and cream on the top. They chose an oil-based paint because they figured it would be more durable than latex for kitchen use.

You Will Need

- Paint
- Primer
- Orbital sander
- Dust mask
- Safety glasses
- Brushes
- Drop cloths

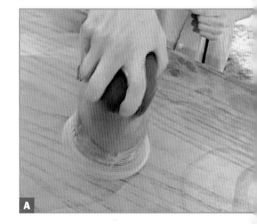

A

1 Before wood cabinets can be painted, the old finish must be removed (but first make sure there's no lead paint, which can't be sanded). Run an orbital sander over the fronts and sides (photo A). Wipe off the dust with a wet rag and let the surface dry.

2 The next step is to prime the cabinets. To possibly save yourself from having to apply a second coat of paint, ask the paint store to use your finish color to tint the primer. Cover the surface with the primer using a brush (photo B). Once that is dry, apply the finish coat.

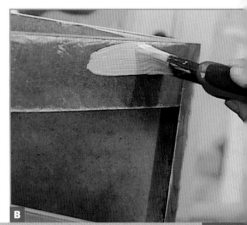

B

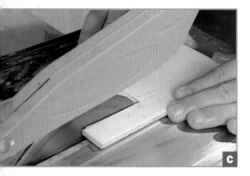

You Will Need

- Tiles
- Premixed mastic
- ³⁄₁₆" V-notched trowel
- Spacers
- Laser level
- Wet saw
- Tile cutter
- Rubber gloves
- Grout
- Grout float
- Bucket
- Sponge
- Cloth rags

TILING THE BACKSPLASH

To stay true to the design of their period house, the homeowners chose white subway tiles for the backsplash, which were installed in a classic brick pattern.

1 Lay the tiles along the length of the wall to see if there will be any short pieces at the end of the run. Once you're happy with the layout, you're ready to set the tiles.

2 Use a ³⁄₁₆-inch V-notched trowel to apply premixed mastic to the wall (photo A). Mastic has a working time of about 30 minutes, so apply it to only a 4-square-foot working area at one time.

3 Set the first row of tiles on the wall. Add spacers between each tile to maintain the proper distance (photo B).

Wiggle each tile a little to spread the adhesive.

4 When you get to an obstacle, such as a light switch, you'll need to make some cuts. Hold the tile up to the wall and make marks where you need to cut.

5 Use a wet saw to make the cut, going slowly and using steady pressure (photo C).

6 For straight cuts you can also use a tile cutter. Simply score the tile along your cut line and press down on the handle to snap the tile in two (photo D).

7 Position the rest of the tiles and let them set for at least 24 hours. Mix the grout according to the directions on the bag. Apply it with a grout float, pushing the grout into the spaces between the tiles at an angle (photo E).

8 Before the grout dries, clean up the excess with a sponge. Keep wiping until the grout on the face of the tiles is gone. Once the grout is dry, there will be a haze on the tiles. Remove it with a rag.

TIPS
DIY Network
Home Improvement

BUY EXTRA TILES
Buy about 15 percent more tiles than you think you'll need in case you accidentally break a few during the cutting process.

WAINSCOT AROUND BANQUETTE

The designer of this kitchen custom-built a banquette seating area that fits snugly in a corner. To complete the hand-crafted look, the home-owners added some detailed trim-work to the wall. The result is a cozy booth to eat breakfast in.

You Will Need

- Eye and ear protection
- Wainscot and trim
- Plywood
- Impulse nailer
- Pneumatic stapler
- Panel adhesive
- Nails and screws
- Level
- Table saw
- Dado blade

1 Put up a ½-inch plywood backerboard to use as a nailer for the wainscot. First apply adhesive to the back, then secure the plywood with a few nails and screws into the studs (photo A).

2 Install a piece of maple as trim for the wainscot (photo B).

3 Along the bottom are boards that have been rabbeted (using a table saw with a dado blade) to receive the ends of the wainscot. Check for level, then fasten them in place with nails.

4 The wainscot is made from medium-density fiberboard (MDF) and will be painted later. Put up pieces of wainscot one at a time. Fasten each piece with a pneumatic stapler (photo C).

5 Cap off the wainscot with a top piece of trim that's also been rabbeted. Check for level, then nail into place (photo D).

6 Use adhesive and nails to attach the edge trim around the banquette (photo E).

A

You Will Need

Faucet

Wrench

B

◢ INSTALLING THE FAUCET ◣

1 Insert the hot-and-cold water valve bodies up through the counter from underneath.

2 Use the escutcheon to gauge the proper height. When the valve body is in the correct position, tighten the connections above and below the counter (photo A).

3 Insert the diverter tee and hand-tighten the nut from below. Then snug the escutcheon over it to hold it in place (photo B).

4 Secure the spout with a retaining ring. First hand-tighten (photo C), and then gently tighten the ring with a wrench.

5 Attach the faucet handles. Use a professional plumber to make the final connections.

TIPS | DIY Network Home Improvement

PROTECT THE FINISH
When tightening the decorative escutcheon, wrap the wrench in tape so you don't scratch the stainless steel finish.

C

◢ INSTALLING THE RANGE HOOD ◣

Installing a range hood may seem intimidating, but it's not that difficult. The manufacturers give detailed instructions on how far up the wall it should be (also check local fire codes), and some even give a template to tape to the wall showing exactly where the holes should be drilled.

You Will Need

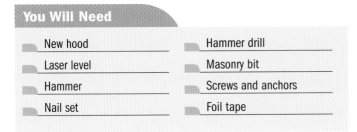

New hood	Hammer drill
Laser level	Masonry bit
Hammer	Screws and anchors
Nail set	Foil tape

1 Determine how far up the hood should be from the cooktop using the manufacturer's recommendations and local code requirements. Use a laser level to mark the center lines from ceiling to counter and between each cabinet. Then, using those lines, tape the template to the wall.

2 Before drilling into the tile, start the hole with a nail set (photo A) to prevent the drill from wandering all over the tile.

3 Use a masonry bit and hammer drill to go through the ceramic tile. If the holes don't hit studs, tap in anchors (photo B), as hoods can weigh about 50 pounds.

4 Attach mounting hooks to the wall (photo C). Hang the hood on the hooks. Once the hood is in place, secure it to the wall with screws.

5 Attach the vent collar to the top of the hood with a few more screws (photo D).

6 Make sure the power is off and then connect the wiring from the wall to the hood vent wires. Call an electrician if you're not comfortable doing it yourself.

7 Cut the vent pipe to length, then slip it over the collar. Wrap the seam with foil tape (photo E) and secure the vent pipe with screws.

8 Finally, the vent cover can be attached to a small mounting bracket screwed into the wall.

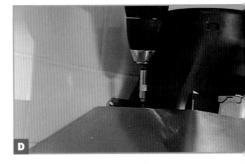

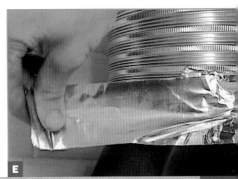

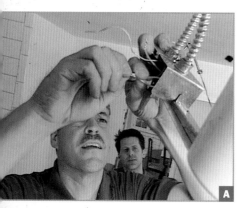

A

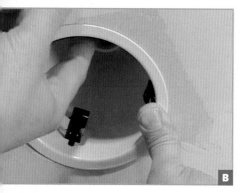

B

C

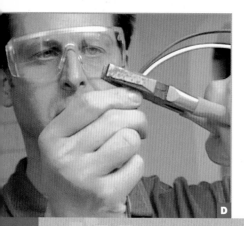

D

◢ INSTALLING NEW LIGHTS ◣

The old kitchen had a large fluorescent light that was overpowering, so part of the new kitchen design called for smaller recessed lights on dimmer switches spread out across the space for highlighting different architectural features. When the new ceiling was put in, a contractor installed all the electrical boxes, so all the homeowners had to do was hook up the wires to the new cans and slide them into place.

You Will Need

- Hacksaw
- Lineman pliers
- Wire nuts
- Mounting bracket

1 Make sure the power is off. Then wire the cans in a series—one wire in, one wire out to the next light. Thread the BX cable into the can and tighten the wire clamp. Connect the wires with wire nuts (photo A).

2 After connecting the wires, put the cover plate on and slide the fixture into the ceiling. Push the four black locking tabs to lock the fixture inside the hole (photo B).

3 Once the ceiling is painted, simply slide the trim plate into the can fixture.

4 To hang a pendant light over the kitchen sink, determine what length the light should be. Manufacturers make these long so you can cut them down to the size you want.

5 After disassembling the light and decorative sleeve and removing the wires from inside, mark and cut both the decorative sleeve and the rod to length with a hacksaw (photo C).

6 Reassemble the light and snip the wires down with lineman pliers (photo D). Then strip the wires and connect them with wire nuts.

7 Put the threaded bar into a standard mounting bracket (photo E). Then slide the decorative cover over the mounting bracket, put in a light bulb, and switch on the power to test.

E

You Will Need

Safety glasses	Clamps
Tape measure	Table saw
Trim	4 x 8 sheets of plywood
Circular saw	Drill
Sawhorses	Router
Lumber for straightedge	Screws
Impulse nailer	Nails
Screw gun	Level
1-by	Pry bar

A

CREATING A BUILT-IN REFRIGERATOR

When people remodel older kitchens, they often find that modern appliances simply don't fit in the space they have. That was the case in this kitchen—the new refrigerator wouldn't fit in the same space as the old one. So the homeowners decided to move the refrigerator to another wall. To give the refrigerator a built-in look, they constructed a shell around it. They used the refrigerator's spec sheet to determine the size of the built-in.

The plan was to create a face frame for the refrigerator out of pieces of plywood, and then finish off the edges. One of the old upper cabinet boxes was reused by cutting down the height and adding to the width to make it fit over the new face frame. Finally, everything got a fresh coat of paint.

1 Since old floors are rarely totally square, take separate measurements for each side panel—one may need to be longer than the other to be flush with the face of the refrigerator.

2 Cut pieces of plywood to size for the two side panels. Use a straight-edged piece of lumber as a guide. Mark the cut line, put the circular saw on the mark, and line up the straightedge with the shoe of the circular saw. Measure the correct distance and set the other edge of the board. Clamp the straightedge down and make the cut (photo A). Once the first cut is made, cut the board to the height of the ceiling.

3 Set the first panel in place and check for level. Jack up the bottom of the panel with a pry bar to make sure it is tight to the ceiling, then nail the first panel to the cabinet (photo B). Secure with screws.

B

TIPS | DIY Network
Home Improvement

CUTTING
To ensure you do not cut through the sawhorses, put a couple of 2 x 4s under the board. Also, make sure that the lumber you use as your straightedge has one side that's actually straight.

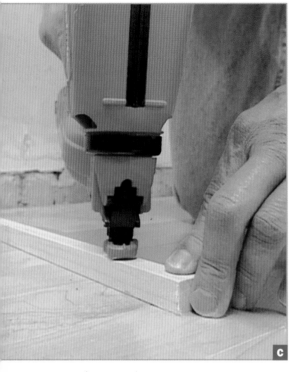

4 Cut a piece of trim and nail it to the panel in order to hide the rough edge.

5 Because the next panel is freestanding (it's not up against any cabinets), use nailing cleats to secure it to the wall and floor. Measure out from the distance of the refrigerator from the side you already installed and draw a line. Cut 1-by cleats and secure the cleats to the wall and floor with nails (photo C).

6 Nail the second panel to the cleats and finish the edge with another piece of trim (photo D).

7 Retrofit the cabinet that used to be above the old refrigerator so it fits over the new one. First make a mark on the wall right above where the top of the refrigerator will be—this is the bottom of the cabinet. Then measure from the ceiling down to that mark to determine how tall the cabinet can be. The width is determined by the refrigerator opening.

8 Use a table saw with its fence set to the correct width to cut the top of the cabinet off. If you were to cut the bottom off, the cabinet wouldn't be as strong. First, lay the cabinet on its back to cut for length (photo E) and then lay it on its side and run it across the saw again to cut for width.

9 Add a new top made of plywood that is ripped to size (photo F). Once it is in place, secure it with an impulse nailer.

10 Use the piece of face frame salvaged from the section of cabinet that was removed to finish the top of the new cabinet.

11 Rip a piece of 1-by to act as fill stock to bring the cabinet out to the correct width. Drill pilot holes and attach the fill with screws (photo G). Then take the retrofit cabinet back into the kitchen, lift it into place, clamp the face frames of the panel and the cabinet together, and finish securing.

12 To make the doors match the modified cabinet, cut an equal amount off

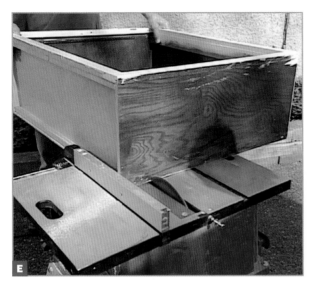

the old doors. Set the fence on the table saw to the correct width and make the cut. Then router the lip so the door fits into the cabinet edge.

13 Now install the new hardware on the cabinet doors, attach the hinges, and put the cabinet doors back in place.

TIPS | DIY Network Home Improvement

FIXING DAMAGE TO CABINETS

If you've gouged your wood cabinets when removing them, don't despair. Simply fix the damage with some rock-hard water putty or another sandable wood filler product. If the damage is on an edge, first create a dam by taping a piece of cardboard to the side of the cabinet. Then, working quickly, use a putty knife to spread the filler material into place. Once the filler is dry, sand, prime, and paint, and you'll never know the cabinet was damaged.

diy network
CONTEMPORARY EXPANSION

This kitchen in a 1950's rambler opened to the family room on one side but a wall separated it from the dining room on the other side, making it a space the homeowners almost never used. The cabinets and appliances were also falling apart, so the plan was to open up the space by knocking down the wall between the kitchen and dining room, then outfit the kitchen with sleek new cabinets and fixtures.

AFTER: The purple and green color scheme provides a cool backdrop to the stainless steel backsplash, new appliances, cherry cabinets, and bamboo floor.

BEFORE: The white kitchen was too cramped, it was separated from the adjacent dining area, and it didn't suit the style of the homeowners.

◀ PROJECT SUMMARY ▶

Architects designed a new plan to expand and unify the kitchen with the rest of the house. First, the old space was torn down to the studs. Unfortunately, the homeowners discovered some water damage which they had to stop and deal with (see pages 160-161). Once that problem was solved, new bamboo flooring was installed to tie the dining and kitchen areas together. The new floor, combined with a new lighting plan and stainless steel backsplashes, makes the space much brighter. Honed granite counters and stock cherry cabinets with glass panels tie everything together. A mix of deep green and purple paint on the walls and new stainless steel appliances complete the contemporary look.

The new kitchen is a great space for entertaining. It's large enough to have several cooks working at the same time, and the cooks can still be part of the conversation happening in the dining room now that the wall between the spaces is gone.

You Will Need

Safety glasses	Speed square
Work gloves	2 x 4s
Hammer	Pry bar
Circular saw	Chalk line
Level	Tape measure
Impulse nailer	Pencil

◢ FRAMING THE NEW WALL ◣

When the old cabinets were removed, the homeowners discovered that a chimney pipe ran up the wall. Since it couldn't be moved and a double-oven was going to go right in its place, the only option was to fir out the wall to bring it to the depth of the chimney pipe. You'd use the same steps to frame a wall that is not firred out.

1 Snap a chalk line out from the existing floor plates (photo A) to indicate the front of your new wall.

2 Lay the 2 x 4s you'll use as top and bottom plates on the floor and temporarily nail them together so you can mark the studs more quickly. Make the first stud mark at 15¼ inches and then 16 inches apart down the plates to ensure that the drywall pieces fall into the center of the studs. Use a speed square to transfer the marks onto both boards at once on the sides of the plates where you will put the studs (photo B). Once the boards are marked, pry them apart to create the spacing for the studs.

3 Lay 2 x 4s out between the top and bottom plates and then crown them (pick each one up and look to see if they are straight or bowed, photo C). If they are bowed, make sure they're bowed in the same direction across the wall.

4 Lift the wall into place (photo D) and secure the bottom of the frame to the subfloor by putting a couple of nails in every other stud cavity.

5 After the bottom is nailed in, plumb the wall and nail the top of the frame into the joists above. Use a pry bar and a hammer to nudge it into place if it's a tight squeeze.

◣ INSTALLING A BAMBOO FLOOR ◢

Bamboo flooring is a beautiful and environmentally friendly choice. This renewable material looks like wood but is actually a grass that regenerates every three to five years, as opposed to wood, which takes about 25 years to regenerate. Bamboo is also extremely durable—as hard as oak or maple. Before installing the bamboo, the homeowners had to prepare the subfloor. They made sure the nails were below the surface, filled gaps larger than ⅛ inch with skim coat, sanded down the high points, and covered the entire area with rosin paper.

You Will Need

- Knee pads
- Tape measure
- Pencil
- Laser level
- 2 x 3 batten board
- 18-gauge pin nailer
- Pneumatic stapler
- Mallet
- Pry bar
- Spline material
- Wood glue

1 Start by finding a reference line off the longest and straightest wall in the room. Use a laser level to mark the line. Then nail a 2 x 3 batten board all the way down the laser line (photo A), which will act as a guide to lay the first board against and ensure that you install the first few rows in a straight line.

2 Lay the first floorboard against the batten board and secure it with an 18-gauge pin nailer, driving the nail right into the shoulder of the tongue (photo B). The nail needs to go in at an angle so it isn't in the way of the next board.

3 Stagger the seams for a more natural look and to give the floor more strength.

4 Once you have a few rows installed, you will be far enough from the batten board to use a pneumatic flooring stapler. Use the mallet included with the stapler to tighten the boards, then nail them into place (photo C).

5 Remove the batten board so you can start working in the other direction. To reverse the direction, you'll first have to retrofit the row to accept the groove of the floorboards. Glue a piece of spline into the groove to create a tongue that will allow you to install rows from that side to the wall.

TIPS DIY Network Home Improvement

MAKING SURE IT'S STRAIGHT
To double-check that your boards are running straight, lay a piece for the second course, line it up with a seam, and push it into place. A tight seam means your lines are straight.

A

B

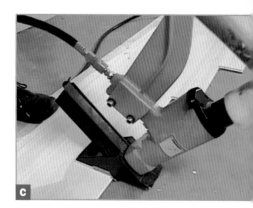

C

INSTALLING NEW LIGHTS

The location of downlighting is critical to a successful lighting plan. The recessed-can lights have to be in the right places, and you need enough of them so that the lighting overlaps; otherwise you'll be left with areas in shadow. This plan calls for 12 new downlights on a dimmer switch and a few pendant fixtures for task lighting.

You Will Need

Laser level	Dimmer switch box
Tape measure	Right angle drill with forstner bit
Staple gun	Wiring
Hammer	Electrical tape
1" screws	Wire cutter
Drill	Wire nuts

1 Make a reference line for each row of recessed can lights. Measure out to the edge of where one light will go, make a reference mark at that line, then go to the other end of the room and make a mark at the same distance out from that wall. Use a laser to create a reference line that passes through both marks.

2 To install a mounting bracket between the ceiling joists, adjust the position of the fixture until your reference laser line runs just along the edge of the opening of the mounting bracket (photo A). The bottom edge of the mounting tabs should be flush with the bottom of the ceiling joists.

3 Tap the mounting tabs into the joist to hold the fixture temporarily in place. Then drive 1-inch screws through all four brackets to hold it securely (photo B).

The brackets slide between the joists so you can adjust where the light will be.

4 Once all the boxes are up, it's time to wire them. Determine the wiring you will use. In this project, 12-2 romax was used. The 12 refers to the gauge, and the 2 refers to the two insulated conductors and a ground wire. The gauge refers to the thickness of the wire. The thicker the wire, the heavier the

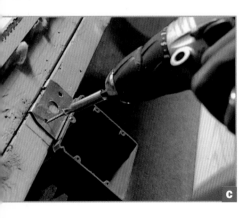

TIPS | DIY Network Home Improvement

HIRE A PRO
While a homeowner can save money by doing the rough wiring, it's best to have a professional electrician make the final connections to the wires that lead to the main circuit panel.

load it can carry. This wire can carry the 20 amps of power these homeowners currently need, and it could handle more in future expansions. Consult an electrician to determine the right type of wire for your project.

INSPECTIONS

Once the new lights are wired, they must be inspected by the local building department before you close up the ceiling with drywall.

D

5 Turn the main power off, and then wire the pendant light. Attach the switch box to the stud (photo C, previous page). The typical height for a switch is 42 inches from the floor.

6 Drill holes through the ceiling joists to run the new line. To make it easier to drill between the ceiling joists, use a heavy-duty right-angle drill with a forstner bit that's big enough for the wire to pass through without binding.

7 Pull the wire through the drilled holes, working from one end of the circuit to the other (from the switch box to each fixture it will control). Leave at least 8 inches of extra wire and coil it inside each box (photo D).

8 Staple the wire to the studs within 8 inches of the box and within 8 inches of where it goes into the wall (photo E).

9 Move on to wiring the series of can lights. Run a length of wire from one can to the next, leaving plenty of excess at each can.

10 To run wires through the can fixtures, twist out a knockout tab in the housing with a screwdriver and insert a box clamp (photo F). Run both wires through the box clamp and strip the ends.

11 Connect the wires with wire nuts—black to black (the hot wires), white to white (the common or neutral wires), and ground to ground wires (photo G). Wrap electrical tape around the wire nuts.

12 Continue wiring the rest of the can lights and bring the wire down to the switch locations.

13 Once the drywall is in place, you can finish the installation. Snap the reflective trim onto the housing of the fixture.

14 Push the fixture into the ceiling, screw in a light bulb, and turn the power back on.

E

F

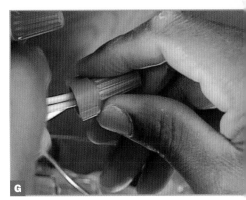

G

◀ METAL BACKSPLASH ▶

A stainless steel backsplash with a diagonal pattern adds a modern look and will also brighten up the space by reflecting the light. The homeowners sent their kitchen design to the manufacturer, so the backsplash came with precut holes for the outlets and finished edges.

You Will Need

- Work gloves
- Construction adhesive
- Putty knife
- Laser level
- Tape measure
- Caulk gun

1 The back of the panel has rows of tape with a peel-off backing, but because the panel is large and heavy, it's wise to add some premium construction adhesive. Spread out the adhesive with a putty knife, making sure it's even and smooth (photo A, top left).

2 Once the stainless steel is prepped, determine where you want the backsplash to start and have a second person point a laser line at that height (photo B, bottom left).

3 Take off the tape's peel-off backing and press the backsplash against the wall.

◀ INSTALLING THE CABINETS AND COUNTERTOPS ▶

These stock cabinets are well made and have dovetail construction and solid cherry doors. The lower cabinets have full-panel doors, while the upper cabinets have glass doors. The homeowners began by installing the base cabinets so the countertop fabricators could measure for and install the countertop.

1 Set the cabinets in place and level them front to back, shimming if needed to make sure they are even.

2 Secure the cabinets to the wall with 3-inch cabinet screws (photo A, top right). Once all the base cabinets are in, you're ready for the countertops.

3 The Brazilian granite countertops are honed, meaning they aren't polished and therefore don't shine. The cutouts for the sink were made at the shop because the edges needed to be polished, but the cutout for the drop-in cooktop was done on site with a circular saw with a diamond blade (photo B, bottom right).

You Will Need

- Cabinets
- Level
- Shims
- Drill
- Silicone
- Screws

4 A bead of silicone secures the granite in place.

◀ INSTALLING THE VENT HOOD ▶

This new vent hood is attractive and powerful. Contractors installed the tube through the ceiling to the roof, where they also installed a cap. The homeowners planned ahead and added backerboard behind the drywall to support the weight of the vent.

You Will Need

- Vent hood
- Drill
- Level
- Vent template
- Flex vent
- Aluminum tape

1 Use a level to mark where the bottom of the vent will be, which in this case was flush with the adjacent cabinets. Mark the center point between the upper cabinets, then line up the template that comes with the vent on the marks (photo A).

2 With the template in place, screw in the hanging brackets (photo B).

3 Hang the vent on the brackets (photo C). Use the leveling screws to align the vent and secure it in place.

4 Take off the junction box cover and make the wiring connections. Make sure the power is off before wiring. If you are not comfortable doing the wiring yourself, it's better to hire a professional. Once the wiring is hooked up, put the box cover back on.

5 Install the ceiling bracket that will hold the duct cover. This mounts flush to the ceiling with mounting screws (photo D).

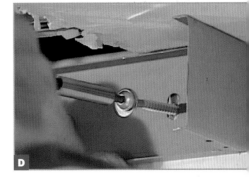

6 Put the flex vent on the transition piece (photo E), stretch it to the vent in the ceiling, and tape the seams with aluminum tape.

7 Put on the duct cover and screw it in place.

A

SINK INSTALLATION

An 18-gauge stainless steel sink with sound-deadening material built in beneath the bottom is a durable and attractive choice. Normally with an undermount sink you have to mount the sink before the countertop goes in. But the granite fabricators channeled some grooves under the counter so the carriage bolt and clip system could be attached after the counter was in place.

You Will Need

- Work gloves
- Undermount sink
- Carriage bolts and clips
- Silicone

1 Six carriage bolts (photo A) will hold the sink in place.

2 Run a bead of 100 percent silicone around the flange of the sink (photo B). Make sure the sink and counter are clean to get full contact with the silicone.

3 Grab the sink by the drain openings and lower it at an angle through the countertop opening. Then pull up to make contact between the counter and the silicone (photo C). Tighten the carriage bolts from underneath.

B

C

INSTALLING GLASS DOOR INSERTS

Stock cabinets are shipped with the doors and glass inserts separate so there's less chance of them breaking. Putting the glass into the door frames is an easy process with the right tools.

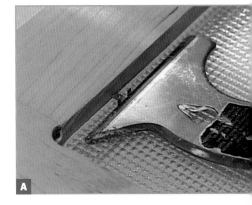

You Will Need

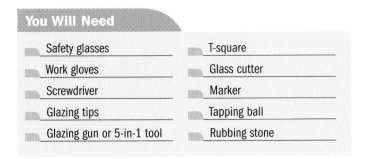

Safety glasses	T-square
Work gloves	Glass cutter
Screwdriver	Marker
Glazing tips	Tapping ball
Glazing gun or 5-in-1 tool	Rubbing stone

1 Remove the cabinet doors from the boxes and set them down on a flat, solid surface. Use glazing tips to hold the glass to the wood frame. You can do this by hand using a 5-in-1 tool to push the tips into place (photo A).

2 Or use a glazing gun to automatically push the glazing tips into the wood (photo B). Put in about 12 per cabinet.

3 If you accidentally break a glass panel or need to cut them down to size, follow these instructions. Mark your cut lines on the glass panel. Use a T-square and a glass cutter with a carbide wheel to scribe the glass. Run the cutter across the width of the glass (photo C).

4 Put the tapping ball side of the glass cutter under the scribe, apply a bit of pressure, and the glass will snap in two (photo D). Do the same thing for your vertical cut. If it doesn't break in a straight line and there is a small shard on the edge, use the teeth on the end of the glass cutter to break the remaining piece off and smooth that portion with a rubbing stone.

TIPS | DIY Network Home Improvement

ORDER EXTRA GLASS

It's a good idea to order extra panes, just in case any are damaged during shipping or installation.

diy
network

48-HOUR SOUTHWEST STYLE

This home was already filled with the warm, earthy tones of the Southwest. There was just one problem: the kitchen didn't fit in. While the homeowner tried to add some color by painting the cabinets, the stark white countertops and appliances stuck out. So she came up with a plan to update her kitchen using rich copper, red-hued eucalyptus, and amber glass.

◣ PROJECT SUMMARY ◥

We installed a new copper vent hood by making some alterations to the cabinets, then we got to work installing two-tone art glass panels in the doors of the upper cabinets separating the kitchen from the eating area. This adds great color and texture and allows more light into the space. The cabinets were finished off with new copper knobs. A eucalyptus hybrid countertop adds even more color and texture. With some finishing touches, such as new appliances, copper backsplashes, a copper sink, and weathered copper faucets with wood handles, this kitchen finally works with the rest of the house.

AFTER: A copper hood and backsplash, new wooden countertops, and art glass panels on the cabinets give this kitchen a bright new look.

A

BEFORE: An outdated range and hood added nothing to the look of this kitchen, and the white countertops and backsplash weren't working with the style of the house.

You Will Need

Eye and ear protection	Scroll saw
Work gloves	Glazing gun
Router	Paint
Metal scribe block	Paintbrush
Drill with spade bit	Sandpaper

B

◢ ART GLASS PANELS ◣

The homeowner designed the glass panel inserts using the manufacturer's design software. The inserts arrived just five days after she placed her order. To mount them to her existing cabinet doors, we removed the middle of the doors.

1 Route out a dado on the back of the door and then cut out the excess. Start by making a plunge cut on a router table (photo A). Use the fence as a template so you know when to stop.

2 A scribe block made out of metal helps you draw a uniform cutting line on the front of the door (photo B).

3 Make a plunge cut on the door front with a spade bit. Then cut out the center with a variable-speed scroll saw (photo C).

C

4 Once the center is removed, go back and clean up the corners with the scroll saw. Sand off the edges and touch up the door with paint.

5 When you're done with the cutouts, hang the doors back in place on the cabinets. Then insert the glass panels and use a glazing gun to attach them to the cabinet doors (photo D).

D

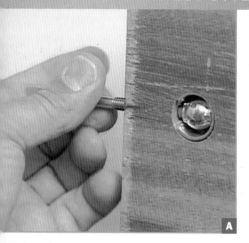

A

◢ INSTALLING BUTCHER-BLOCK COUNTERS ◣

The new butcher-block counters are made out of liptus, a eucalyptus hybrid. Hybrid varieties grow faster than traditional wood, making them an environmentally conscientious choice. While hardwoods like maple and oak take 50 to 70 years before they're ready for harvest, hybrid eucalyptus takes only 15.

You Will Need

- Turnbuckles
- Biscuits
- Wood glue
- Hammer
- 100% silicon
- Small brush

1 Slide the countertops into place over the cabinets. Slip the turn-buckles into the predrilled holes under each section (photo A).

2 Brush wood glue into the precut slots on the side of the countertop where it will meet another section. Then apply wood glue to the biscuits and insert them into the slots (photo B).

3 Slide the countertop segments together until you have a tight seal (photo C), then wipe off any excess glue that seeps out.

4 Under the counter, insert the locking rings into the holes adjacent to the ones that have the turnbuckles (photo D). The locking rings keep the bolts from turning as you tighten the cinch nut of the turnbuckle.

5 Repeat this process until each section of countertop is installed. Run a bead of 100 percent silicone between the counter-tops and the cabinets to hold them in place.

B

C

D

A

B

INSTALLING THE COPPER BACKSPLASH

Copper backsplashes behind the range and sink match perfectly with the new copper vent hood, sink, and faucet.

1 Install a batten board on the wall to support the weight of the backsplash while the adhesive dries (photo A).

2 Apply premium construction adhesive to the back of the backsplash. Make sure the adhesive covers 90 percent of the backsplash. Use a 6-inch drywall knife to smooth the adhesive (photo B).

3 Put the backsplash in place on the wall, applying pressure to the copper to smooth it out and make sure the adhesive bonds to the wall.

4 Install a second batten board over the top of the panel as a precaution until the adhesive dries. Slide a cloth between the board and the backsplash to protect the copper from scratches. Then slip a shim in behind the batten board to increase the pressure, ensuring the adhesive will bond (photo C).

5 Repeat steps 2 and 3 with the sink backsplash. Because it's a smaller piece, it doesn't need the batten boards.

You Will Need

- Batten boards
- Drill
- Premium construction adhesive
- 6" drywall knife
- Cloth
- Shim

C

RUSTIC CONTEMPORARY

The owners of this kitchen were in the middle of a whole-house remodel, and they were eager to get the kitchen done so they and their three small children could finally move into the house. Their plan was to create a kitchen with both rustic and contemporary elements.

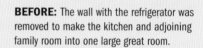

BEFORE: The wall with the refrigerator was removed to make the kitchen and adjoining family room into one large great room.

AFTER: The glass backsplash tiles are a great focal point behind the cooktop. Painted white cabinets above and stained wood below are tied together with the black and white marble countertops. Box beams (shown below) give the ceiling some architectural interest.

◢ PROJECT SUMMARY ◣

The architect came up with a plan to put the refrigerator and pantry on one wall, a sink under the new windows, an oven and cooktop opposite the refrigerator wall, and an island in the center. When I arrived, the kitchen had already been torn down to the studs and the new drywall and subfloors were put into place. We began by installing a Tasmanian oak floor and finish wood-work such as decorative box beams and trim around the windows. Factory custom cabinets gave both homeowners what they wanted: cream-colored cabinets on the walls and wood grain below with special features like a built-in wine rack. A powerful vent hood needed to be installed where none was before, so work was completed both inside and outside the house. Then professionals installed the Guatemalan, kitchen-grade marble counters and integral sinks. Two colors of square and rectangular tiles made from recycled bottle glass brighten up the backsplash. Pendant lights, new appliances with cabinet panel fronts, and a flip-screen unit that allows the homeowners to watch TV, surf the Internet, and even keep an eye on kids in other rooms, top off this stylish space.

The center island has a prep sink and faucet, as well as bar seating. Large windows and a great lighting plan make the space feel bright and open.

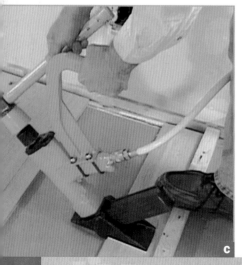

You Will Need

Ear and eye protection	Chalk line
8-penny ring shanks	String
Nail gun	1 x 2 batten board
Rosin paper	Pneumatic floor nailer
Hammer tacker	Compressor
Laser level	Screw gun
Tape measures	Screws
Pencil	House wrap and fiberboard

◢ INSTALLING TAZMANIAN OAK FLOORING ◣

The wide, Tazmanian oak flooring really warms up the space. To make sure your new wood floor won't squeak, the subfloor must be solid. In this case, there were multiple layers of subfloors, so the homeowners started by driving nails across the floor to tighten the subfloor to the joists underneath.

1 Once the subfloor is secure, you can roll out the rosin paper. This acts as a sound barrier under the wood floor. Roll it out, overlapping the pieces by at least 4 inches, and secure it to the subfloor with a hammer tacker (photo A).

2 You need to make sure your new floor will be square, so take your time and double-check your measurements during this step. Set up a laser level across the floor near the center of the room. Measure from the laser to the straight wall at both ends of the room. Line up the laser level across two tape measures to determine the straight line in the middle of the room (photo B). Mark two points along the line with a pencil. Snap a chalk line along these marks. A little hairspray over the chalk line will make sure it won't get wiped away.

3 Screw a batten board (a straight 1 x 2) to the floor along the chalk line about every 2 feet. This will act as a brace for the first course of flooring and prevent it from shifting.

4 Loose-lay several boards until you get the look and layout you want. Then use a pneumatic floor nailer and compressor to nail in the floorboards (photo C).

5 Professionals can be hired to sand and finish the wood floor. To protect it during the rest of the job, cover the floor with house wrap, which is water-resistant and more durable than regular paper, and then cover that with ¼-inch sheets of fiberboard. Cut them to size, lay them out, and tape them together to prevent shifting.

◢ BUILDING BOX BEAMS ◣

To break up the large expanse of open ceiling, the homeowners designed a system of box beams with crown molding that give the room some architectural character. The beams first need to be constructed with pre-primed poplar wood.

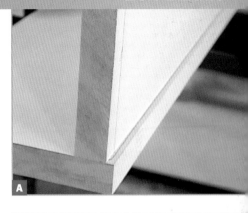

A

1 Cut the boards to length. Using a pencil and a speed square, scribe a line ⅛ inch from the edge of the board to mark the spot for the reveal.

2 Stand one board along the reveal line of the bottom board so the two boards are at a 90-degree angle (photo A). Hold the two boards together with quick clamps until you attach them permanently.

You Will Need

- Pencil
- Speed square
- Pre-primed poplar
- Quick clamps
- Nail gun
- 1½" pin nails
- 2½" screws
- Screw gun
- Painter's caulk

B

3 Use a pneumatic nail gun loaded with 1½-inch pin nails to attach the three cut boards together. Drive nails from below so that the top board doesn't move out of place, and at an angle to prevent the boards from pulling apart. Nail every 6 to 8 inches.

4 Use scrap wood from the earlier cuts to support the final board while you clamp it and then nail it into place (photo B). Fill the nail holes with painter's caulk.

5 Now you're ready to bring the beam up to the ceiling. The first beam should go in the center of your room (if there is a ceiling joist to screw it into there). Use a laser line to guide the placement of the nailer board that you'll attach the box beam to. Use a nail gun to temporarily hold the nailer board and then screw it into place with 3-inch deck screws, making sure you hit the ceiling joist (photo C).

C

6 Place the finished box beam over the nailer board on the ceiling. Nail the beam into the nailer board using 2½-inch finish nails every 6 inches (photo D).

D

You Will Need

- Window trim
- Drill
- Chop saw
- Trim screws (torx head)
- Torx-head driver bit
- Painter's putty
- Nail gun
- 1¼" finish nails
- Wood glue

INSTALLING WINDOW TRIM

1 Cut the sill piece to length. The wood chosen for this piece is very hard, so the homeowners drilled screw holes before putting it into place.

2 Screw the sill into the window frame using trim screws and a torx-head driver bit. These have very small heads, and the torx drive provides better contact on smaller screw heads (photo A).

3 Attach all the trim pieces around the window with 1¼-inch finish nails. A nail gun will speed up this process (photo B).

4 Use wood glue to attach the small finishing ends of the trim (photo C). Putty the countersink holes.

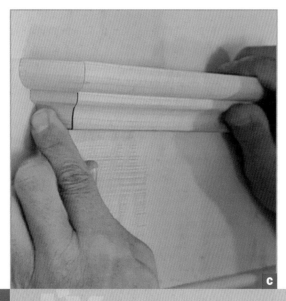

TIPS | DIY Network
Home Improvement

A FLUSH SILL

If your sill piece isn't sitting flush against the window and drywall, you can cut some of the drywall away. Hold the sill piece in position and draw an outline of it on the drywall. Use a utility knife to score the outline, then remove excess drywall with a small chisel.

⚒ INSTALLING THE CABINETS ▶

The homeowners worked with a factory custom cabinet company that provided help with the cabinet design and sent a representative to check the order once it arrived on site. The company was able to pass on the cost savings of its factory setup, so these cabinets ended up costing less than they would have if made by a small custom cabinet shop. The company offered veneers in more than 100 species of wood, giving the homeowners quite a choice in color and character. They settled on an African wood called sapele to cover the lower cabinets, then went with a creamy white paint on the upper cabinets. The rails and stiles on the cabinets are solid sapele, but the boxes are veneer, which saves a lot of money.

You Will Need

- Tape measure
- Laser level
- Straight level
- Pencil
- 1-by for ledger board
- Drill
- Bit extension
- 3" cabinet screws
- Shims

1 Figure out where the bottom of the upper cabinets will be on the wall. Shoot a laser line across the wall and mark several spots. Screw a ledger board into the wall along the line to support the upper cabinets during installation. Make sure the screws hit studs in the wall (photo A).

2 Lift the first cabinet onto the ledger and attach it to the studs in the wall with cabinet screws. If it's difficult to get at the back of the cabinet, use a long bit extension to drive in the screws (photo B). Install the remaining upper cabinets.

3 The factory custom cabinets come with a separate toekick platform rather than having the toekick built into the base cabinets. Use filler strips of wood under the back of the cabinets instead of expensive hardwood flooring. Set the toekick in place and use shims to level it side to side and front to back (photo C). Screw the toekick platform into the studs in the wall using 3-inch screws.

4 Set the cabinet on the platform. Screw the cabinet into both the platform and the wall. Continue these steps until all base cabinets are in place.

TIPS | DIY Network Home Improvement

T-JACKS

For especially heavy pieces, a special cabinet lift called a T-jack can be used to help hold the cabinets at the proper height until the screws go in.

A

B

INSTALLING THE CENTER ISLAND

This island is composed of a variety of separate pieces that fit together like a puzzle.

You Will Need

- Tape measure
- Level
- Tape
- Pencil
- Drill
- Clamp
- Panhead cabinet screws

1 To place the center island, refer to the plans and measure from both the sink wall and cooktop wall. At the intersection, make a mark that represents the center of the island (photo A).

2 Use a level as a straightedge to mark points on each side and put down a piece of tape to indicate where the edge of the base should sit.

3 Set the toekick platform for the island in place using the tape line and center mark as references (photo B) and then set the center island on top.

4 Secure the first cabinet box to the base platform (photo C). Then secure the remaining cabinets with cabinet screws.

5 Clamp the other cabinet boxes together to secure them in place and connect them with panhead cabinet screws (photo D).

6 Attach the doors and slide in the drawers to finish the island cabinet installation.

C

D

You Will Need

Gloves	Keyhole saw
Safety glasses	Hammer
Ladder	Pry bar
Drill	Nail gun
Utility knife	Reciprocating saw

◢ INSTALLING THE VENT HOOD ◣

In most renovation projects, the ductwork for the vent is already in place, but for this project it needed to be installed. Luckily, the new siding hadn't been installed on the outside of the house yet, so all the crew had to do was remove the house wrap and sheathing to expose the framing and the wall. They pulled back the insulation (be sure to wear gloves when touching insulation) and removed a piece of bracing that was in the way.

1 From inside the house, run a keyhole saw through the wall to mark the location of the vent hole (photo A).

2 From outside the house, toenail a piece of blocking in the correct position to hold the hood hangers. This piece of wood will provide more support than drywall alone for the heavy vent.

3 Using the vent elbow as a template, mark the hole placement outside (photo B). Cut a hole through the studs with a reciprocating saw.

4 Finish the hole in the interior drywall and dry-fit the elbow (photo C).

5 Use the paper template provided by the hood manufacturer to mark the location of the hangers and screw them into the blocking piece installed outside the house in step 2 (photo D).

6 After making the electrical connections (while the main power is off), place the elbow in the hole and then slide the vent hood into place, making sure it connects to the elbow and rests on the hangers (photo E).

◢ INSTALLING THE SINK AND COUNTERTOPS ◣

The kitchen counters and sink are made of Guatemalan kitchen-grade marble. Marble is porous and therefore not always recommended for kitchen use, but this particular kind is harder and denser, making it less porous and better able to stand up to heavy use. These pieces are heavy and delicate, so a team of professionals came in to do the work. Before the sink could be installed, a heavy-duty support frame was built to hold its weight from underneath.

1 The installers used 4 x 4 lumber for braces and screwed them into the sides of the cabinet. Then 2 x 4 legs were constructed to fit under the braces (photo A) and were held together with angle brackets.

2 Dry-fitting the sink took a lot of muscle (photo B).

3 Before the installers set the counters in place, they taped off the cabinets to protect them. The multiple slabs were placed, and shims were used to ensure they were flush and level.

4 Seams between the slabs were sealed with epoxy that was colored with pigment to match the stone. Once the color was right, hardener was added and the epoxy color mix was pushed into the seams (photo C).

The tape on each side of the seam protected the stone.

5 While the epoxy dried, the crew caulked the edges along the bottom of the countertop (photo D). Then tape was removed and the excess epoxy scraped away.

6 Next the sink countertop was dry-fit. The installers left a ¼-inch reveal around the sink (photo E). Once the sink was positioned, they lifted the countertop, applied a bead of silicone around the edges, and put it back in place.

7 Homeowners can apply an enhancer-sealer to the countertop. The enhancer brings out the color, and the sealer protects the stone. It will need to be applied every one to three years, or when spills aren't wiping up as easily.

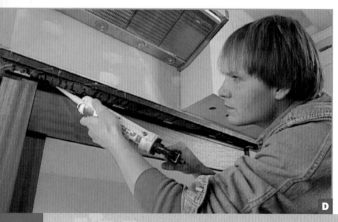

A

You Will Need

- Light fixtures
- Screw gun
- Wire nuts
- Wire stripper
- Fine-tooth hacksaw

INSTALLING PENDANT LIGHTS

Two pendant lights over the island and one over the sink add task lighting to this kitchen. Make sure the main power is off before you start work. If you have any hesitation about electrical work, hire an electrician. In this kitchen, the boxes were already installed in the ceiling, so we just had to install the fixtures.

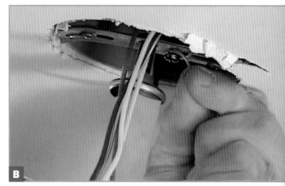
B

1 Screw the threaded mounting bracket over the box to hold the fixture (photo A).

2 Wrap one ground wire around the green screw on the bracket (photo B).

3 Attach the other ground wire to the free end of the first ground wire and put on a wire nut (photo C). The light will now be grounded.

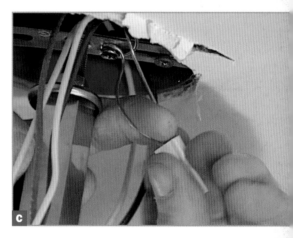
C

4 When you twist two wires together, leave both a little long. Then go back and cut both wires in the middle of the twist (photo D). This creates a perfect thread for a wire nut. If you can see bare wire outside the wire nut, you have stripped too much insulation and you will have to start over again.

5 Connect the rest of the wires, white to white and black to black.

6 If you need to shorten the light fixture, use a fine-tooth hacksaw to cut the outside shaft and the threaded rod.

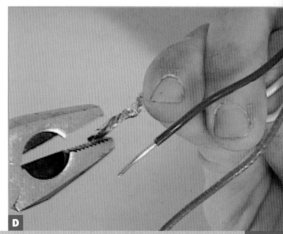
D

A

B

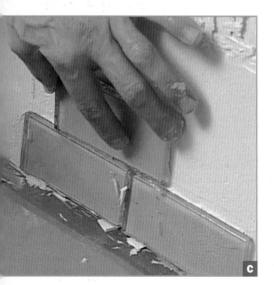

C

You Will Need

Glass tiles	Thinset
Work gloves	Modified grout
Safety glasses	Disposable gloves
Wet saw with diamond blade	Rosin paper
Dry cloth	Painter's tape
Margin trowel	Bucket
Spacers	Drill with paddle mixer
Rubbing stone	Float
³⁄₁₆" square-notched trowel	Sponge

TILING THE BACKSPLASH

The glass tiles for the backsplash are handmade from recycled bottle glass. The homeowners chose rectangular green and square amber-bronze tiles. With glass tiles, you'll be able to see any imperfections on the wall, so be sure the surface is smooth before you install them.

1 Mark the center of the backsplash area. Then apply thinset adhesive to the wall with the flat side of a ³⁄₁₆-inch square-notched trowel. Don't apply more than you can tile over in five minutes. Use the notched side of the trowel to comb through the thinset at a 45-degree angle, which gives you ridges of the proper thickness. Then smooth over the thinset to get rid of the comb mark (photo A); otherwise, you'd see them through the glass tile. Try to do this without changing the depth of the thinset on the wall.

2 Use a dry cloth to wipe each tile clean. Then, with a margin trowel, apply thinset to the back of each tile (photo B). This technique is called back buttering.

3 Set each tile in place and wiggle it to make sure there are no air pockets in the thinset (photo C). Use spacers to make sure the tiles are set in a uniform pattern.

4 To cut the glass tiles, use a wet saw with a diamond blade. The cut edges are razor sharp, so use a rubbing stone to smooth them.

5 Continue placing tiles in the desired pattern across the wall.

6 Before grouting the tiles, lay down rosin paper to protect the counter, taping the seams to the edges of the tile.

7 Mix modified grout with water using a paddle mixer. Modified grout has polymers in it that help prevent shrinking and cracking. Let the grout slake (rest and thicken up) for about 10 minutes, then stir again until it reaches the consistency of peanut butter.

TIPS | DIY Network Home Improvement

GROUT COLORS

Choosing grout colors is just as important as choosing tile colors. Decide whether you want the tiles to stand out or blend together. In this case the homeowners went with a neutral color to accent the glass tiles.

D

E

8 Using a float, apply the grout at a 45-degree angle. Make sure to really work the grout in between the spaces (photo D). Use a margin float to get grout into tight corners. Don't worry if the grout looks darker than you expect; it will lighten as it dries.

9 After letting the grout set for 15 to 20 minutes, sponge away the excess at a 45-degree angle to the grout joint, being careful not to pull any grout out of the joints (photo E).

HIGH-TECH ADDITION

There are rustic and contemporary elements in this unique kitchen, and to top it off the homeowners wanted a television, computer, CD/DVD player, and radio—but they didn't want all the clutter each unit would bring. The solution was a product that incorporates all these elements into one compact unit. The installation is simple.

A plate on top of the box attaches with bolts under a cabinet, and the screen flips down for viewing. The unit comes with a paper template, which assists in positioning the screws for the mounting brackets. To navigate the screen, you have the option of the keyboard, the remote control, or the screen stylus. The keyboard has a waterproof seal. You can even hook up a closed-circuit camera to keep an eye on your children in other rooms while you're cooking.

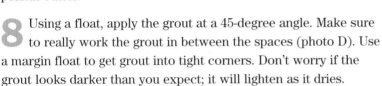

48-HOUR CABIN

The owner of this vacation cabin in the woods had been working on it every weekend for five years. He'd had enough of cooking on a hot plate outside and was more than ready for the new kitchen.

PROJECT SUMMARY

This 1929 cabin was about to be torn down when the homeowner found it. In order to transfer it to his homesite in the woods, he had to carefully take it apart, move the pieces, and reconstruct the cabin using the notes he made during the deconstruction process. It's a small, three-room structure, but when it was put back together, the roof was raised to give it a more open feeling. The kitchen had been updated in the 1960s with orange cabinets and laminate counters. Before I arrived, the homeowner had already

AFTER: Stainless steel appliances and light wood cabinets brighten the cabin and provide modern amenities.

cleared out the old kitchen and laid new slate tiles. The goal was to create a space that worked with the look of the cabin but that included modern amenities. Light wood cabinets are a nice contrast to the dark logs, and the maple butcher-block counter keeps the woodsy theme going. The kitchen was finished off with modern stainless steel appliances and a faux deer antler chandelier.

BEFORE: Paul and the homeowner were able to get right to work since they had a blank slate to start with.

You Will Need

- Wood trim
- Table saw
- Impulse nailer
- Nails

TRIMMING OUT THE DOORS

Before the new cabinets could be installed, the door to the kitchen needed to be framed. We used some wormy cyprus wood from another part of the original cabin for this purpose. You can find salvaged wood from a variety of sources to give your project a unique look. Reclaimed lumber often costs more, but you can't put a price on the character it brings to your home.

1 Run each piece of wood through the table saw to trim to size. In this case, the boards were originally tongue-and-groove, so the tongues needed to be cut off to create a smooth edge (photo A).

2 Fasten them to the door frame with an impulse nailer (photo B).

A

B

135

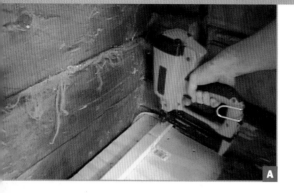

◄ INSTALLING THE CABINETS ►

Light maple cabinets brighten up the space. In older homes, subfloors are often uneven, making installing floors and cabinets more difficult. But in this case the homeowner firred up the floors before laying the slate tiles, so he knew that the cabinets would go in evenly.

1 The first cabinet is a tall unit, so the homeowner ordered it without a base, figuring it would be easier to install the base separately, get it level, and then attach the large cabinet to it. The floor tiles don't reach all the way to the wall, so a long, narrow shim was nailed to the subfloor against the wall so the base would sit level (photo A).

You Will Need

- Level
- Drill
- 2⅜" panhead cabinet screws
- 2 x 4
- Shims
- Tape measure

2 Set the base in the corner, secure it to the wall, and shim with 2⅜-inch panhead cabinet screws (photo B).

3 Lift the cabinet onto the base, check it for plumb, and screw it to the wall (photo C).

4 Next in line will be a dishwasher, but if you measure for the dishwasher and keep installing base cabinets down the rest of the wall and find out the cabinets won't fit in the end, you'll have to cut into the new cabinets. To avoid that, Paul and the homeowner decided to start on the opposite side of the wall and work toward the dishwasher. That way, they could fill the area around the dishwasher with trim stock if needed.

5 To hang the upper cabinets, screw a piece of 2 x 4 lumber into the wall to act as a temporary ledger. Set the cabinet onto the 2 x 4 and check for level and plumb. Shim the back if the walls aren't even, as is the case in this log cabin. Then secure it in place using the 2⅜-inch panhead cabinet screws (photo D). Continue installing the rest of the cabinets along the wall.

▬ INSTALLING THE COUNTERTOPS AND SINK ▬

Butcher-block counters used to be available only in maple, but now you can get them in a variety of woods. This homeowner decided to stick with maple, though, to match his cabinets.

1 Flip the counter over so that if the saw blade causes any damage it will be to the bottom. Measure the space where the countertop will be installed, transfer that measurement to the underside of the counter, and cut off the excess. For thick, hard wood, like butcher block, you need heavy-duty power tools. Use a wormdrive saw with a new, sharp blade to make this cut (photo A).

You Will Need

- Butcher-block counter
- Tape measure
- Eye and ear protection
- Pencil
- Wormdrive saw
- Saw blade
- Sink
- Straightedge
- Scrap wood
- Screws
- Drill
- Right-angle drill
- Auger bit
- Jigsaw

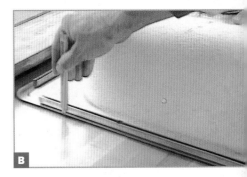

2 Once the counter is in place, you can install the sink. Flip the sink over so you can trace around it for the cutout (photo B). Make sure it's centered over the cabinets below, and at an even distance from the front and back edges of the counter.

3 The cut line should be recessed 5/16 inch from the outside line that you trace, so the sink can be dropped in and rest on the lip. Use a straightedge to mark that line.

4 Before making the cut for the sink, install a piece of scrap wood over that section so that the cut piece won't fall through prematurely and rip the counter. Attach the scrap with one screw in the center of the cutout and spin it as you go to avoid cutting it along with the counter (photo C).

5 Use a heavy-duty right-angle drill with an auger bit to make a hole in each corner of the area to be cut out (photo D).

6 Make the straight cuts with a wormdrive saw (photo E). Run the blade from one hole to the next in each corner. Finish the edges with a jigsaw.

7 Dry-fit the sink to make sure it fits inside the cutout. Hire a plumber to make the final sink connections.

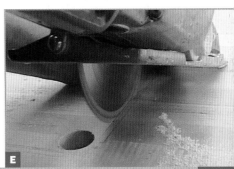

A

You Will Need

Fill stock	Wall brackets
Circular saw	Drill
Table saw	Pin nailer
Screws	Decorative molding

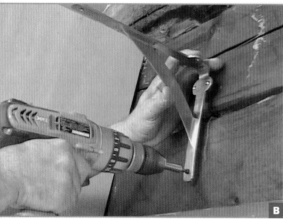

B

INSTALLING THE SHELF ABOVE THE SINK

To fill in the empty area above the sink between the upper cabinets, the homeowner constructed a shelf with some of the fill stock that came with his cabinets.

1 Mark the fill stock and cut it down to size (photo A). The homeowner also cut some decorative molding pieces that came with the cabinets to add to the base of the shelf.

2 Screw three stainless steel brackets into the wall (photo B). These will match the stainless steel appliances in the kitchen.

3 Set the shelf in place on top of the brackets and pin-nail the decorative molding to the face (photo C).

TIPS
DIY Network
Home Improvement

FILL STOCK
Always order plenty of extra fill stock and molding from your cabinet manufacturer. Not only does it hide gaps between boxes, but it can be used for additional projects like this one, and you know the finishes will match.

C

INSTALLING THE LIGHTING

The bare light bulb hanging from the center of the kitchen just wouldn't cut it in this newly remodeled space. It was replaced with an antler chandelier made of a composite material that looks like the real thing.

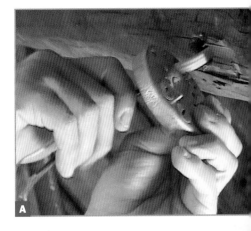

You Will Need

Antler chandelier	Grounding wire
Electrical box	Wire strippers
Drill	Wire nuts
Screws	Electrical tape

1 Make sure the main power is turned off before starting any electrical work.

2 Secure a shallow electrical box to the log (photo A). The wires run through the log and to the main service panel. This light fixture didn't come with a grounding wire, so the homeowner secured one right to the box.

3 Connect the light fixture's wires to the wires in the box with wire nuts (photo B). Then put the decorative cover in place, add chandelier bulbs, and switch on the power to test.

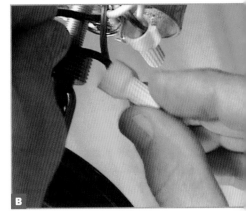

IMPROVISING

When you live out in the woods, you have to be resourceful. Luckily, the homeowner had a friend with a skid loader that could lift the big appliances up the unpaved pathway and to the cabin (as shown at right). The homeowner had to remove a patio door to get the appliances into the cabin, as the front door wasn't wide enough.

diy network

CHERRY AND GRANITE

For 14 years, the owners of this home paid more attention to raising their kids and working than to home improvement projects. Slowly they began updating other rooms of the house, and eventually it was time for the kitchen. They took a sledgehammer to the room and remodeled it from top to bottom.

BEFORE: An island that didn't fit the space (above), tired cabinets and countertop (below), and an odd configuration left the homeowners cold.

AFTER: The mix of granite counters and cherry cabinets warms up the new kitchen. Stainless steel appliances and sink, all in the right spots, make working in this space a breeze.

This project came together with gorgeous granite countertops that the homeowners installed themselves, rich cherry cabinets, and an island that accommodates both a cooktop and bar seating for four.

PROJECT SUMMARY

After developing a plan with a kitchen designer, we emptied the kitchen and started tearing out the old cabinets, countertop, and tile floor, busting through the pantry wall to gain some valuable space for the new island. Porcelain floor tiles that look a lot like natural slate provided a neutral base for the stock cherry wood cabinets. An electric in-floor heating system will make sure the tile stays nice and toasty.

An L-shaped island with a cooktop on one side and bar seating on the other makes the most of the space. And a unique do-it-yourself granite countertop installation saved a lot of money and provided a classy finish to the room. We finished it off with new paint, low-voltage pendant lights, and stainless steel appliances.

You Will Need

Mask and gloves	Pry bar
Safety glasses	Hammer
Plastic (for doorways)	Reciprocating saw

REMOVING AN INTERIOR WALL

The wall of the pantry needed to be removed to make more room for the kitchen island. Before you take down an interior wall, make sure it's not a load-bearing wall. If you are uncertain, consult an architect, certified building engineer, or your local building department. You technically can remove a load-bearing wall, but the job is best handled by professionals. Cover the entryway with plastic to keep dust from spreading. Also be sure the power is turned off at the circuit box before knocking through the drywall.

1 Use a hammer to knock holes in all of the stud cavities to check for what's inside (photo A). Electrical receptacles in the wall are a good indication that there are wires running through the wall. Carefully work around them.

2 Once you have several lines of hammer holes, put your gloved fingers into them and rip the drywall off the studs.

3 When the wall is down and the wiring exposed, have a licensed electrician look at the configuration and make any changes needed. When the wires are out of the way, pull the studs down. Use a hammer to pop them out at the top and bottom (photo B) and they should slide right out.

4 The corner post of this kitchen was solid wood, so it wouldn't be smart to pound it out. Instead, it's best to use a reciprocating saw to cut through it (photo C) and then remove the pieces.

5 Next, the top and bottom plates of the wall need to be removed. Carefully work around any electrical receptacles. Use a pry bar to remove the plates.

6 When you rip the top plate down, you may lose some of the ceiling (photo D), but it can be patched with new drywall. Be sure to wear a mask, especially during this step, as you never know what could fall from behind the ceiling.

A

IN-FLOOR HEATING SYSTEM AND SUBFLOOR

Before laying the new tile floor, the homeowners chose to install an electric in-floor heating system. Each brand has its own instructions, but this system is made out of semiconductive plastic strips with two low-voltage wires on each side. The wires heat up the middle of the strips, but there's no current there, so you can even nail through the middle section when installing a floor over it. This is a relatively easy project for do-it-yourselfers. Just send your kitchen floor plan to the manufacturer, which will provide you with all the materials and tools you need.

1 Roll out strips of thermoplastic polymer across the floor and make cuts with scissors (photo A). Staple the strips to the subfloor.

2 Connect terminal wires to the end of each strip. Black (positive) and white (negative) wires are connected from one strip to the next, then to the terminal board and transformer. Start by cutting a small corner of the plastic element to expose the braided wire that runs the length of each strip. Slip the metal connector over the braided wire at the heating strip (photo B).

3 Insert the flattened terminal wire into the connector so the two wires are touching (photo C). Use the special crimping tool that comes with the system to crimp the connector so it's tight.

You Will Need

- Gloves and eye protection
- In-floor heating kit
- Scissors
- Wires
- Connectors
- Sealant tape
- Terminal boards
- Transformer
- Crimpers
- Stapler
- Thinset
- Bucket and sponge
- Trowel
- Cement backerboard
- Power nailer
- Galvanized 1¼" roofing nails

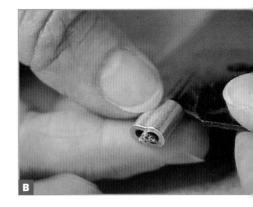

B

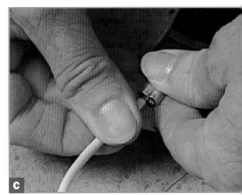

C

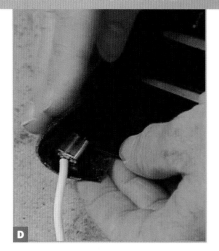

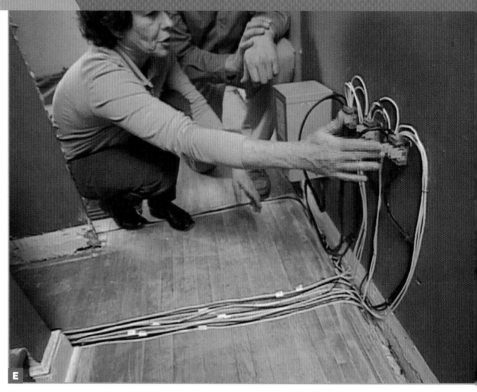

4 To finish the connection, cut a short piece of sealant tape, fold it in half, peel away the backing, and wrap it around the connection (photo D). Press out the air to form a permanent seal.

5 Route all the wires into terminal boards and then to the transformer box and call an electrician to install a switch. In this case, the homeowners were able to put these components in a closet, where they would be out of sight (photo E). Test that the system works before proceeding.

6 Now that the heating elements are in place, create a smooth surface over them before laying the tile. You can do this by placing cement backerboard over the heat system.

7 Mix a portland-based thinset with water. Before you apply the thinset, eliminate the possibility of nailing through any of the terminal wires by marking the backerboard so you will know where the wires are.

8 Use a trowel to apply the thinset mortar on top of the heating elements. The grooves created by the trowel will help hold the backerboard in place.

9 Lay the backerboard on top of the mortar. Leave a small gap between each board to allow for expansion and contraction. Use a power nailer with galvanized 1¼-inch roofing nails to secure the boards (photo F), and then don't walk on the floor for 24 hours.

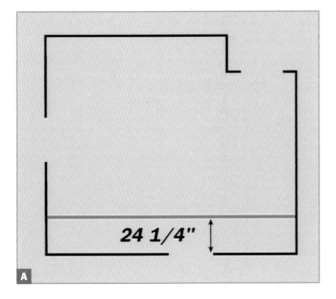

24 1/4"

A

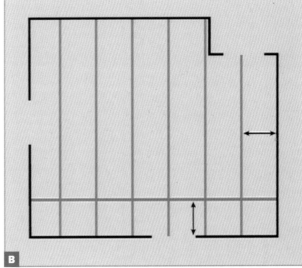

B

INSTALLING PORCELAIN TILE

These Italian-made porcelain tiles look a lot like natural slate. The surface color goes all the way through the tiles, so if you chip one, it won't be so noticeable. This floor should also be easy to keep clean. Remember to wear gloves and eye protection when working with concrete products.

1 Before you start installing the tiles, you must create a grid. Do this by laying out three tiles and measuring the width of two tiles, with grout joints included, to determine the square size for the grid.

2 Figure out the width of two tiles with a space for grout between them, in this case, 24 ½ inches. Then measure the same distance out from the longest wall and mark that measurement on the subfloor several times across the room (diagram A). Once you have your marks, snap a chalk line.

3 Mark the grid from a second wall and snap another chalk line. Then mark the lines all the way across the room (diagram B). Lay out four tiles within one of the grid boxes. If you keep the tiles in the grid boxes and center them evenly, you should not have to use spacers.

4 Mix the thinset mortar to the consistency of peanut butter. Apply a thin layer over the cement backerboard using a ¼ x ⅜-inch deep square-notched trowel (photo C). Try to get even coverage, and don't cover your grid lines. Apply thinset to one grid box at a time.

You Will Need

- Bucket and sponge
- Drill with mixing paddle
- ¼" x ⅜" deep square-notched trowel
- Sanded grout
- Grout float
- Cotton rag
- Thinset
- Chalk line
- Measuring tape
- Wet saw

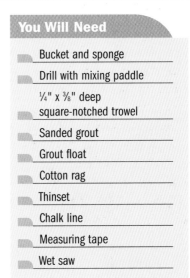

C

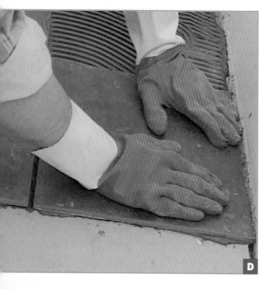
D

E

F

5 Apply a thin layer of mortar on the back of each tile and spread it with the flat edge of a trowel.

6 Set the tile in the thinset and apply pressure with both hands (photo D). Make sure all the tiles are set at the same level.

7 Stop to clean up any excess thinset on the face of the tiles and in the grout lines with a damp sponge after laying tiles in each grid box. Be sure to squeeze all the water out of the sponge before wiping the surface.

8 Use a wet saw to make cuts (photo E). Don't force the tile through or apply too much pressure, or the blade will bind and make a bad cut.

9 Continue laying tiles across the floor. When you have to fit small pieces along a wall or in a corner, it can be difficult to apply thinset to the floor. In this case, just apply the thinset to the backs of the small pieces and set them in place.

10 After the tiles have set for 24 hours, apply the grout. For this project, the homeowners chose a dark grout, which will hide dirt better than a light color would. They chose a sanded grout to add body to the mixture and help keep it between the tiles during the application. Mix the grout according to the directions on the bag. Grout dries quickly, so don't mix more than you can use, as you won't be able to add more water later.

11 Pour some grout over the tiles and use a grout float held at a 45-degree angle to push it over the tiles and into the joints (photo F). Remove most of the grout on the first pass.

12 Let the grout set for a few minutes until it starts to dry on the face of the tiles, and then go back over it with a sponge. If you wait too long, you'll have a harder time getting the grout off the face of the tiles. But if you don't wait long enough, you'll pull the grout out from between the tiles. Wipe slowly with a smooth, steady motion, rinsing the sponge in clean water frequently. Once all the grout is dry, wipe off any remaining haze from the tiles with a cotton rag.

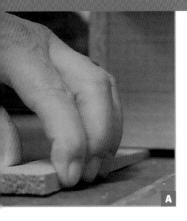

A

B

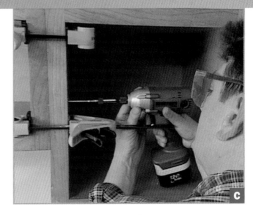

C

◢ INSTALLING THE CABINETS ◢

The homeowners chose stock cabinets with a cherry wood finish, which gives them a sleek look and much more storage space. When stock cabinets arrive, check your order against the packing list and make sure you have all the components you need. Also check that the doors open in the right direction. This can take some time, but it's best to do before you begin the installation.

You Will Need

- Safety gear
- Tape
- Drill
- Impact driver
- Stainless steel deck screws
- Level
- Rubber mallet
- 2-by lumber
- Shims
- Clamps
- 1¼" screws

1 Start in a corner and build out from there. It's crucial to make sure the first cabinet is plumb and level, because if it isn't, none of the others will be. Remove the cabinet doors to make it easier to attach cabinets to each other, and mark where the doors came from.

2 Hold the first cabinet in position and slide a couple of shims under the bottom if needed to adjust for level (photo A). Check for level from front to back and side to side.

3 Drill pilot holes through the back of the cabinet, making sure you hit the cleat the manufacturer put behind the unit. Drive 2-inch panhead wood screws that came with the cabinets into the wall stud. Use an impact driver, which won't strip screws like a regular drill might.

4 Lift the next upper cabinet into place and clamp it to the top of the pantry on one side while a helper holds up the other side. Check it for level (photo B) and make adjustments as needed with a rubber mallet.

Once it's in the right spot, screw it to the wall studs, going through the back cleat.

5 Now that it's attached to the wall, further secure it by screwing the face frames of the first two cabinets together (photo C). Drill pilot holes 1 to 2 inches from the top and bottom of the corner cabinet. Then countersink the pilot hole to hide the head of the screw. Use a ¼-inch bit with tape wrapped partway around it so you can watch to see that you don't drill too far through the wood. Drive 2-inch stainless deck screws through the face frames.

TIPS | DIY Network Home Improvement

ORDER OF WORK

Install the lower cabinets first if you have an intricate design or a tall unit in the corner. Otherwise, install the upper cabinets first so you don't have to reach over the lower ones.

6 To give the refrigerator a built-in look, the homeowners added a side panel. The panel needs to sit flush with the cabinet box above the refrigerator, but there's a gap in the back. Insert a spacer block at the back of the upper cabinet to supply something solid to screw the side panel into (photo D). Nail in the spacer block and then attach the side panel to the upper cabinet's face frame as in step 5.

7 On another wall of the kitchen, there's a spacing problem. The microwave is 19 inches deep, but the cabinets surrounding it are only 12 inches deep, so a pair of box beams will need to be installed behind the cabinets to build them out to 19 inches. This way, the microwave will be flush with the cabinets. A panel will be used to hide the box beams on the side.

8 Construct the box beams out of four pieces of 2-by lumber. Screw three sides together with 3-inch deck screws and then screw the two three-sided boxes into the top of the wall for the upper cabinets, making sure you hit the studs. Once the beams are in place on the wall, add the fourth side (photo E).

9 Attach the cabinets for this wall as you did in previous steps. In this kitchen, the soffit at the top of the wall wasn't level, so the homeowners installed this wall of cabinets as one unit. They

attached the cabinets together first, then lifted and attached them to the wall.

10 When you connect two stock cabinets, sometimes there's a ½-inch gap, which hinders your ability to screw the units together. Insert shims between the cabinet boxes to eliminate the gap. Clamp the shims into place and attach the units by screwing through the shims with 1¼-inch screws (photo F). Then score the shims with a utility knife and knock the excess off with a rubber mallet.

11 Make a T-brace to hold the upper cabinets up as you make sure they are plumb and flush with the wall (photo G). Use shims as needed and secure the unit to the wall, again through the cleats in the back and into wall studs using 3-inch screws.

You Will Need

Grinder	Duct tape	Caulk gun
Buffer	Circular saw	Toothpicks
Granite cutter	Dry-cut segmented diamond blade	Painter's tape
Dyes	Eye and ear protection	Polyester-based resin
¾" plywood	Dust mask	Pigments
Drill	Spade bit	Rubber gloves
Vix bit and screws	Jigsaw	1" putty knife
Builder's paper	Sink	Cardboard and craft paper
Utility knife	2' and 6' levels	Mixing plate
Carpenter's square	1¼" screws	Rags
Two long 2 x 4s for cutting support	Screwdriver	Seam stone
Sawhorses	Clear silicone	Caulk

DO-IT-YOURSELF GRANITE COUNTERTOPS

Most granite countertops need to be professionally fabricated and installed, but the homeowners found a company that would cut and ship the slabs in sections for homeowner installation. They sent final plans of the kitchen to the manufacturer, which cut the sections to size and shipped them about four weeks after the order was placed. All of the counters come with a prefinished bullnose edge and are ¾-inch thick so that they can be lifted by one or two people. Make sure you have some help when the slabs arrive, as some pieces can weigh more than 200 pounds. Handle them with care throughout the process. The manufacturer can cut out the sink hole in advance and also supplies you with the materials you need for the installation.

A

1 Prepare the tops of the cabinets by installing sheets of ¾-inch plywood. This gives the counter a stable base and raises it high enough to allow for the bullnose edge overlap, which otherwise would prevent the drawers from opening. Make sure the plywood does not overhang the outside edge of the cabinet.

2 Attach the plywood to the frame of the cabinets with screws, making sure to center the screws into the frames underneath (photo A). Drill a pilot hole first to keep from splitting the hardwood face frame.

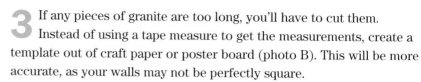

B

3 If any pieces of granite are too long, you'll have to cut them. Instead of using a tape measure to get the measurements, create a template out of craft paper or poster board (photo B). This will be more accurate, as your walls may not be perfectly square.

4 Apply a piece of duct tape over the granite so you can see your cutting mark, then use a circular saw with a dry-cut segmented diamond blade to make the cut (photo C). Always wear a dust mask plus hearing and eye protection when cutting granite.

5 Test-fit the cut pieces and be careful with long, thin pieces that could snap. In this kitchen, the sink needed to be installed underneath the counters, so once the counter had been dry fit, it was removed again so the sink could be installed. Before removing the counters, trace the opening for the sink onto the plywood (photo D). The sink hole seen here was cut by the manufacturer.

6 Use a spade bit to make a pilot hole through the plywood, then use a jigsaw to cut the sink hole (photo E). Make it about ⅛-inch larger than the line you drew so there's room to drop in the sink. Dry-fit the sink.

7 The next step is to secure the countertop to the plywood underneath, but first check to make sure the plywood pieces are level. If they aren't, use 1¼-inch screws to adjust the height of the slab from underneath (photo F, next page), which will raise and lower the countertop. You won't harm the underside of the countertop; the screws will just push up on it enough to make the seams meet up.

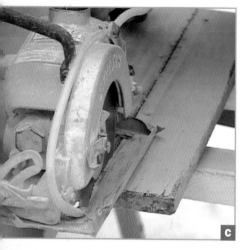

C

8 Lift the granite again and put dollops of silicone around the perimeter of the cabinets and in the center of the counter, spaced about every 6 to 12 inches (photo G, next page). Run a bead of caulk around the sink rim. Apply a second bead of caulk on top of the sink rim to waterproof the gap between the sink and countertop. Gently lower the granite slab back down.

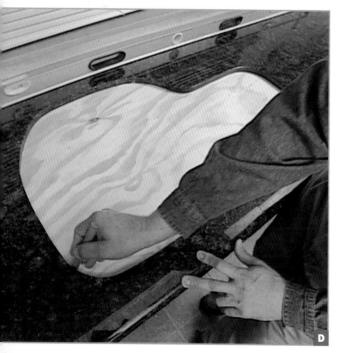

D

E

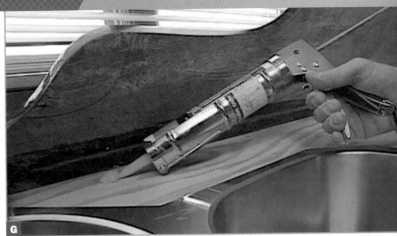

9 Fill in the seams between pieces with a mixture of poly-ester-based resin and colors from the manufacturer. Add color to the resin a little bit at a time. Mix with a putty knife and keep checking the color against the stone (photo H). With multicolored stone, the seams will blend better if you combine about three colors in each seam.

10 Once your colors are ready and the seams have been taped off with painter's tape, add hardener to the col-ored resin using 3 percent hardener to 97 percent resin. Mix only a workable amount at a time, as you have about five min-utes before it hardens.

11 Apply a basecoat of the neutral color to the seam. Dab it in and smooth it as you go. Then apply a little of the lighter color here and there, and apply some of the dark-est color last (photo I).

12 As soon as you're done, pull off the painter's tape so the resin doesn't dry on the tape. It takes about 30 minutes to dry completely.

13 Once the resin is dry, smooth it out with a seam stone attached to a cordless drill (photo J). Use a low speed and firm pressure. Keep the stone moving in small circles and you'll feel when the seam is smooth.

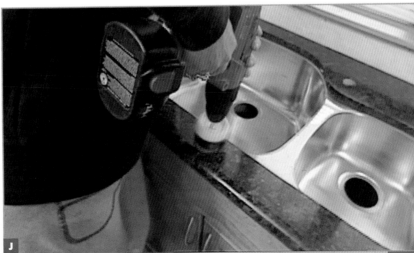

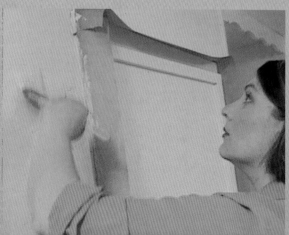

3

Basic Techniques

This chapter gives detailed information on the techniques needed to get your kitchen remodel rolling. Here you'll learn how to demolish your existing kitchen, patch and paint walls, install appliances, and more. You'll also find tips on living without a kitchen during the construction process and on getting rid of debris responsibly.

Finally, keep the instructions, owner's manuals, and any other reference materials that come with the particular products you intend to install. Start a folder that is easily accessible so you can go back and double check facts and figures along the way.

O.K., let's build that kitchen!

Paul

You Will Need

- Safety glasses
- Work gloves
- Wire cutters
- Pry bar
- Hammer
- Reciprocating saw
- Circular saw
- Painter's tape
- Drill and bits

DEMOLITION

Before doing any demolition work, be sure to protect yourself. Wear pants and long-sleeved shirts, heavy gloves, and goggles to avoid injury from flying debris. If you're using a loud power tool, wear earplugs. And if you're removing walls or floors, wear a respirator so you don't inhale too much dust. Use extreme caution when cutting into walls and floors so you don't hit any pipes or wires.

◀ REMOVING CABINETS ▶

1 If you're keeping the cabinet boxes and drawers and painting, or otherwise altering them, remove the doors and drawers and make notes about where they go in the kitchen. They may all look the same, but sizes can vary. Write the location of the drawers on the backs, where no one will see them (photo A). For the doors, write on pieces of painter's tape stuck to the inside face.

2 To remove upper cabinets, first take off any molding pieces with a pry bar (photo B).

3 Unscrew and remove the cabinet unit in one piece if you plan to reuse it (photo C).

4 Unscrew the old cabinet doors by removing the hinges (photo D).

5 Before removing cabinets around the sink, turn off the shutoff valves under the sink or the main water supply to the house. That way, if you accidentally hit the water supply pipes and they break, you won't have a flood on your hands. Disconnect the plumbing under the sink and take out the sink with a pry bar.

6 Hire a plumber to cut the copper water-supply line to the refrigerator, turn off the main gas line to the stove, and disconnect the supply line at the back of the stove.

A

B

C

D

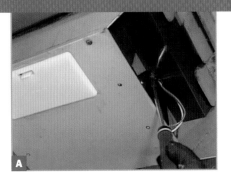

REMOVING A VENT HOOD

1 Be sure to turn off the power before removing the vent hood. Then unscrew and remove the access panel (photo A).

2 Once you're sure the main power is off, snip the wires (photo B). Use the wire nuts from the hood vent to temporarily cap off the wires if you will use them again for the new hood.

3 Screws hold the hood in place. Unscrew them and release the hood (photo C). The portion of the vent housed in the upper cabinets can be removed along with those cabinets during the demolition process.

You Will Need

- Screwdriver
- Wire cutters
- Wire nuts
- Gloves

TIPS
DIY Network
Home Improvement

REUSE AND RECYCLE CENTERS

Before you start demolishing your kitchen, check to see whether your community has a building materials reuse or recycling center. Some centers accept intact cabinets and doors and will give you a donation receipt so you can take a tax write-off. The centers then sell your items to other homeowners and builders who are renovating older homes. Materials like tile, drywall, plaster, plumbing, and wiring can be taken to building recycling centers and made into something that someone else can use. So don't just add to the landfills—recycle what you can.

SETTING UP A TEMPORARY KITCHEN

Most major kitchen renovations take about eight weeks to complete, which is a long time to be without a kitchen. It's a good idea to set up a temporary kitchen someplace else in the house, such as in a basement, garage, laundry room, or spare room. If there isn't any existing counter space, set up a folding table with a small microwave, toaster oven, crock-pot, and coffeepot. Have a few utensils, cups, and plates on hand, and keep usage of paper plates and plastic utensils to a minimum. If you're lucky there might be a utility sink nearby. If not, you'll be washing dishes in a bathroom sink. Make sure to scrape off all food before rinsing, as non-kitchen sinks aren't equipped with garbage disposals. A large tray will help you cart dishes to the sink. Another good idea is to use sheets of paper to cover your makeshift counter while preparing food. Once you're done, just throw the paper away.

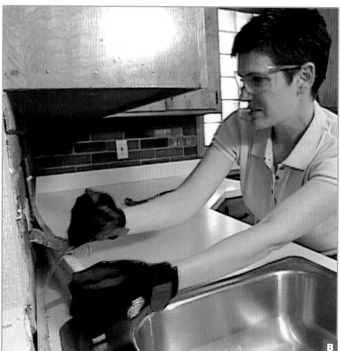

REMOVING A COUNTER AND BACKSPLASH

1 Use a circular saw to make cuts through the top of the counter to make the pieces more manageable (photo A).

2 Use a pry bar and hammer to remove the old backsplash (photo B).

3 If you're tossing the sink, just disconnect it from the water supply and drain pipes then lift it and the surrounding counter up in one piece.

TIPS | DIY Network Home Improvement

GETTING RID OF OLD APPLIANCES

Who will take your old refrigerator, range, and dishwasher? If your appliances are still in good working order, check around to see if you can donate them to a local charity. If not, you will have to take them to your local dump and pay them a fee to dispose of them.

REMOVING APPLIANCES

1 Make sure to unhook the gas line before moving the stove out. Use an appliance dolly and have enough helpers.

2 Measure the exit route to make sure the appliances will fit. You may need to remove the refrigerator door.

You Will Need

Heavy gloves		Take-up shovel
Eye and ear protection		Utility knife
Circular saw		Pliers
Pry bar		Floor scraper

A

REMOVING A VINYL FLOOR

1 If you have layers of vinyl flooring to remove, it's easiest to do it in one step. Score the floor with a circular saw (photo A, above right). Set the blade to the depth of the floor layers without cutting through the subfloor and the joists. Cut an X pattern in the floor so you can get your pry bar under the layers in several areas.

2 Once you've lifted an area with the pry bar, use a take-up shovel to remove large pieces of flooring. These are commonly used for roofing work and have points on the end.

3 If you have just one layer of vinyl flooring to remove, score it in sections with a utility knife to make it easier to pull out. Use pliers and wear gloves to ensure a better grip, then pull up the largest pieces possible. You may need to use a scraper to get up tough areas.

TIPS | DIY Network Home Improvement

RENT A TRASH BIN
You will probably have a large amount of construction debris to get rid of. Depending on the scope of your remodel, you may need to rent a trash bin to dispose of any materials that cannot be recycled. Check with your local garbage service to see which construction materials cannot be disposed of in this way.

REMOVING FLOOR TILE

If you want to save and reuse floor tiles, cut around the grout lines with a rotary tool and use a pry bar to remove each piece. If you don't want to save them, and you want to remove the tiles but not the subfloor, it's much quicker to smash them. Place a towel over the tiles so the shards don't fly across the room, and then hit the tiles with a hammer. Be sure to wear eye protection and heavy gloves. A hand scraper will remove any remaining adhesive from the floor.

If you need to remove the tiles and subfloor, cut out 2-by-2-foot sections, use a pry bar to lift each piece up (photo A, below left), and remove the floor one section at a time (photo B, below right).

A

B

You Will Need

- Drop cloths and tarps
- Bucket of water and dish soap
- Scoring tool
- Special wallpaper-removal cloths
- Putty knife
- Sponge

◀ REMOVING WALLPAPER ▶

1 Prep the area by throwing down drop cloths. Then mix a bucket of warm water with a generous amount of dish soap (the soap helps the removal sheets stick to the wall).

2 Use a scoring tool like the one shown here (photo A) to make cuts in the wallpaper. Simply run the tool up and down over the surface of the wall.

3 Soak the wallpaper-removal sheets in the bucket of soapy water and slightly ring excess water out. Apply the sheets to the wall leaving a ½-inch gap between them (photo B).

4 Leave the sheets on the wall for about 45 minutes and then remove them.

5 Peel off the wallpaper (photo C). Some backing may remain on the wall, but it will scrape off easily with a wide putty knife.

6 While the wall is still wet, and once all the wallpaper is off, wipe down the wall with a wet sponge and the rest of the glue should come right off.

You Will Need

- Drop cloths/plastic sheeting
- Masking tape
- Respirator
- Safety goggles
- Heavy gloves
- Screwdriver
- Wire snippers
- Electrical tape
- Utility knife
- Pry bar
- Reciprocating saw
- Backsaw
- Shop vacuum

A

◢ REMOVING AN INTERIOR WALL ◢

Before removing any wall, make sure it is not load-bearing. If you don't know, have a structural engineer examine it for you. Load-bearing means that the wall is supporting part of the weight of the house. While a load bearing wall can be removed, it's best done by a professional who can take extra precautions to support the weight. The following instructions are for removing a non-load-bearing wall.

1 Shut off the circuit breakers that control any electrical receptacles or fixtures in the area you'll be working in. Then make sure there is no power going to those receptacles or fixtures.

2 Protect the floor with drop cloths. Cover or remove furniture in the room. Tape heavy plastic sheeting over the doorways and vents so that fine dust does not travel throughout the house.

3 Unscrew receptacle cover plates and remove the switches or receptacles. Cut the wires leading to the fixtures and wrap the ends with electrical tape.

4 Wear safety glasses and heavy gloves. With a utility knife, score the top of the wall where it meets the ceiling. If the wall you're removing connects to a door or window, first remove the trim.

5 For drywall, locate an area of the wall that's between studs and punch through with a pry bar or hammer (photo A). Use the clawed end or your hands (photo B) to tear out pieces of drywall from there.

B

TIPS | DIY Network Home Improvement

LATH AND PLASTER SAFETY GEAR
Invest in a respirator to protect your lungs from tiny dust particles and lead that may be in plaster walls. If you're removing a plaster wall, consider wearing a body suit with an integrated hood to cover your body and hair.

6 If you have lath-and-plaster walls, remove the plaster first and then the lath. Hit the plaster with the clawed end of a pry bar to create a hole, then slide the flat end of the pry bar between the plaster and the lath and push up to remove it. Then remove the lath with the clawed end of the pry bar.

7 After the wall surfaces are removed, roll up any electrical wires toward the ceiling and tape them securely out of the way. If there is any plumbing in the wall, cut off the pipes at the floor and cap or reroute them. Make sure the water is shut off first.

8 Once wires and pipes are removed, you can cut out the wall framing with a reciprocating saw. Cut through the middle of the studs, then grab each piece and pull it back and forth until it separates from the top or bottom plate.

TIPS | DIY Network Home Improvement

THE QUICKER WAY

If you are absolutely certain there are no electrical wires or plumbing in the wall you want to remove, you can skip a few steps and cut through the whole thing with a reciprocating saw. If you're not sure, don't risk it.

You Will Need

Plastic suit	Fan	Pressure sprayer
Respirator	Hammer	Bleach
Gloves	Garbage bags	Scrub brush
Eye protection	Tape	Mop
Plastic sheeting	Vacuum	
Hammer tacker	Putty knife	

DEALING WITH MOLD

When the owners of this kitchen pulled up the subfloor, they found that it was wet underneath along one wall. Another clue that the wall was wet was that the paint wasn't adhering to it.

They brought in a contractor, who used a wet-wall detector that can read moisture up to 3½ inches deep inside the wall cavity. A second device, a pen-type tester with longer probes, actually goes into the wall and determines the per-cent of moisture inside. There is also a do-it-yourself way to detect moisture. Drill a hole in the wall to put in a desiccant (silica gel) spike that you can purchase at home centers. Once it's inside the wall, cover the top with tape. Check it several hours later. If the desiccant has changed from yellow to green, then you have a moisture problem and possibly mold.

Since you won't know what the mold situation in the wall is, take extra precautions before removing the drywall. Seal off the entire area with plastic sheeting and set up a fan that will blow air from the room outside. Wear a plastic suit, protective eyewear, a respirator, and gloves to be safe.

1 Once you're ready to go, tap a row of holes in the drywall with a hammer and break it off with your hands in chunks. Remove the insulation, put it in garbage bags, and tape them shut to keep the mold contained. Look for mold growing on the studs and framing. If you don't have more than about 2 square feet of mold, you generally don't have a health hazard—but you will need to clean up the mold.

2 In this case, the mold wasn't so bad and all the homeowners had to do was clean out the wall cavities and then let the area dry for a few days. If the mold seems extensive, call a professional to help you remove it.

3 Once you have the drywall out, you should be able to tell what direction the water is coming from. Be sure to solve whatever problem caused the water damage right away.

4 Remove any loose dirt with a putty knife and vacuum. Spray the base of the studs and the floor using a pressure sprayer with a mixture of 50 percent water and 50 percent bleach, which will kill any living organisms (photo A).

5 Let the bleach mixture soak in, and then scrub the area with a stiff brush (photo B).

6 Remove excess liquid with a mop and let the area dry completely before installing new subflooring and drywall (photo C).

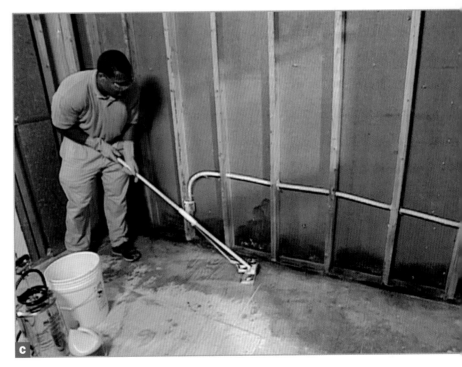

anatomy of a wall

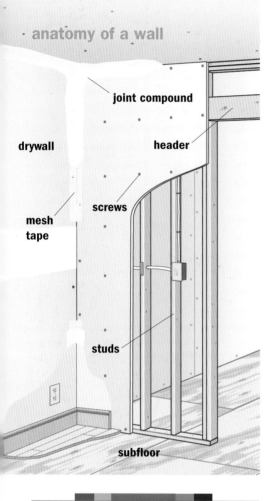

joint compound

drywall

header

screws

mesh tape

studs

subfloor

TIPS | DIY Network
Home Improvement

INSTALLING A SUPPORT BRACE

Drill a screw into the center of the support brace so you have something to hold on to as you screw each side in place. When the support is secure, remove the center screw.

WALLS

You Will Need

Carpenter's square		Joint compound	
Pencil		Taping knife	
Drywall saw		Fine sandpaper	
1 x 3 lumber		Circular saw	
Drywall screws		Drill	
Self-adhesive fiberglass tape			

PATCHING DRYWALL

Small dents and scratches in drywall can be filled with joint compound or spackle, then sanded and primed. If you have a popped nail, pry it out and use a drywall screw to fasten the drywall to the stud. If the existing nail won't come out or you would cause more damage by removing it, countersink the nail and drive a drywall screw right next to it for added support. Be sure the head of the screw sits just below the surface of the wall so it dimples the drywall paper but doesn't rip it. Then cover with several coats of joint compound, sand, and prime. Small holes can be patched with joint compound, then sanded and primed. If you have a hole between 3 and 12 inches across, use the method below.

1 Use a carpenter's square to mark straight lines around the damaged area, as it's much easier to patch a hole with straight sides. Cut out the damaged area with a drywall saw.

2 If the hole is between studs, you'll need to add a support brace to which the new piece of drywall can be attached (see tip). Cut a piece of 1 x 3 lumber about 8 inches longer than the hole's width. Put the lumber into the wall and hold it as you drive drywall screws on each side of the hole into the lumber, countersinking the screws.

3 Measure the hole and cut a new piece of drywall to fit. Attach the new piece of drywall to the support brace with countersunk drywall screws.

4 Apply fiberglass mesh tape to the seams.

5 Spread joint compound over the mesh tape with a taping knife. Feather the edges to reduce the amount of sanding you'll have to do. Let the joint compound dry, then sand it smooth with fine sandpaper, and apply a second coat. Sand the second coat when it is dry, and then prime before painting.

◢ PATCHING PLASTER ▶

Most repairs to drywall also work for plaster walls, with some exceptions. Fine cracks and nail holes can be filled with spackle. Holes up to a few inches can be filled with either drywall joint compound or patching plaster. If you cut a large hole in the wall and go through the lath, the easiest way to patch it is with a piece of drywall. Get a piece the same thickness as your current lath-and-plaster wall. If the hole is at the ceiling or floor, you can attach the drywall piece to the framing. If not, cut over to the nearest stud and attach the drywall piece to that.

1 If you're starting with a rough hole, draw lines around the perimeter (photo A) to make it a square or rectangle. Make sure the hole goes to the nearest stud.

2 Use a circular saw to plunge-cut into the wall (photo B). This will give you relatively straight, clean edges to work with.

3 Cut a piece of drywall to fit the opening with a drywall saw or utility knife. Attach the drywall patch to the studs with 2-inch drywall screws (photo C).

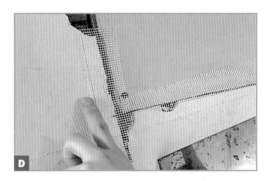

4 Apply pieces of the fiberglass mesh tape to span the gap between the plaster wall and the drywall patch (photo D).

5 Use a small taping knife to apply a thin layer of joint compound over the mesh tape (photo E). Feather the edges. If you don't end up with a smooth coat, let it dry, sand it lightly, and apply a second coat. Sand the second coat when it is dry, then prime and paint.

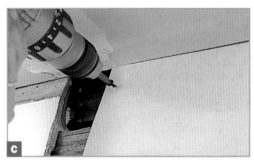

cut-in

patched area

TIPS | DIY Network
Home Improvement

PREPARING THE ROLLER

New rollers often have a lot of lint that can make marks on your wall. Run the roller over a few pieces of taut masking tape to remove the lint before you use it.

PAINTING

You Will Need

Drop cloths	Painter's tape
Grease-cutting cleanser	Paint and primer
Bucket	Small paintbrush
Sponge	Paint tray
Rags	Roller kit
Screwdriver	Ladder (if needed)

◢ PAINTING A WALL ◣

Preparing to paint takes much more time than painting, and doing it carefully is the key to a good paint job. Always buy the highest-quality paint you can. It will adhere to the wall better and possibly save you a second (or third) coat.

1 Protect your floors and furniture with drop cloths. Remove any window treatments and rods. Remove receptacle and switch covers and lighting fixtures. Tape off any areas you don't want to paint, such as baseboard or window molding. If you're replacing molding and trim, remove it before you paint the walls.

2 Wash the walls with a grease-cutting cleanser and look for cracks or holes. Patch any holes and replace any loose plaster (see pages 162–163). Once you have a flat, smooth surface that's free of dust and dirt, you're ready to paint.

3 Paint one wall at a time to avoid lap marks (these appear when you let a wet edge dry and then paint the rest of the wall later). First cut in at the ceiling, sides, and floor. Cutting in means outlining the area by painting it with a brush rather than a roller.

4 To cut in (photo A, next page), hold the brush at the base rather than at the handle for more control. Place the tips of the bristles almost to the edge of the wall. Then, when you start to apply pressure, the bristles will expand out toward the edge. You want only the very tips of the outer bristles to touch the edge so you can control the amount of paint.

5 Cut in only as much area as you can finish with a roller before the paint dries. Have the roller and tray ready to go before you cut in. Dip the roller into the deep end of the tray and then roll it back and forth over the grated section to saturate the roller evenly.

6 Roll an M shape in the upper corner (see illustration on previous page). Then, without reloading the roller, fill in the area. Roll slowly and bring the roller as close to the edges as possible (photo B) to mask the different texture of the area you cut in with a brush. Reload the roller when you think it is removing paint from the wall rather than adding it. Paint one 3-by-3-foot section at a time.

A

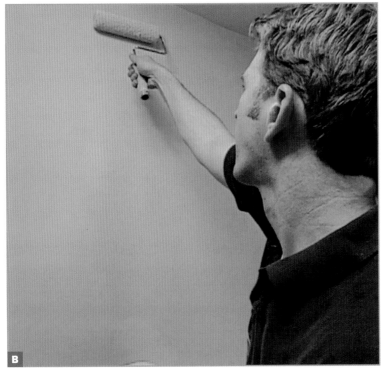
B

TIPS   DIY Network
        Home Improvement

LADDER SAFETY

▥ If you need to use a ladder when painting a wall or ceiling, be sure it's set on a stable surface.

▥ Never reach when you're on a ladder. Always take the time to get down and move it over to avoid a reach.

FIXTURES AND FINISHING

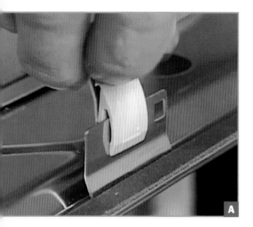

◢◣ INSTALLING A DROP-IN SINK ◢◣

You Will Need

▸ Screwdriver

▸ 100% silicone

1 Start by attaching the mounting clips that come with the sink to the bottom edges (photo A).

2 Some sinks, like the one shown here, have a foam gasket that eliminates the need for silicone (photo B). If your sink doesn't have a foam gasket, run a bead of silicone along the lip of the sink.

3 Set the sink in place on the counter. From underneath, tighten the retaining clips to the counter (photo C).

MOVING A REFRIGERATOR

Refrigerator wheels only go two ways—forward and backward—so a special tool like this airlifter will protect the floor and the backs of the people installing particularly heavy models. Two pads slide under the refrigerator, and once they're in place, the blower hose shoots air into the pads. Be sure to brace the refrigerator during this step so it doesn't tip over. The blower hose is equipped with a valve that regulates the flow of air. Open the control valve all the way. Once the air is flowing, start closing the valve to keep the pads from filling too quickly. Gently guide the unit through the room. Make sure to keep it level, not putting too much weight on either pad. Take your time. Once the unit is lined up, slide the pads out. Then use the refrigerator wheels to roll it into place.

You Will Need

- Drill
- Reciprocating saw
- Wood blocks

◢ INSTALLING A COOKTOP ◣

1 Drill two access holes into the cabinet underneath the cooktop, one for wiring and one for gas (photo A).

2 Dry-fit the cooktop and modify the cabinet back if needed with a reciprocating saw (photo B).

3 Use wooden blocks to test-fit so that your fingers don't get caught under the lip (photo C). Once the cooktop is in place, remove the blocks.

TIPS | DIY Network Home Improvement

DRY-FITTING APPLIANCES

If you have professional plumbers and electricians coming to make the final connections on your appliances, always dry-fit the units first. It may be difficult to make modifications once they are hooked up.

A

B

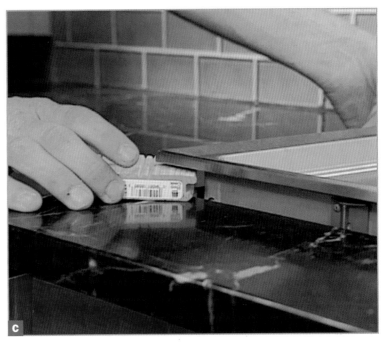

C

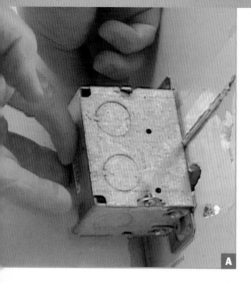

A

You Will Need

Hammer	Screwdriver and drill
Pry bar	Jab saw
Eye protection	Remodel electric box
Tape	Tin snips

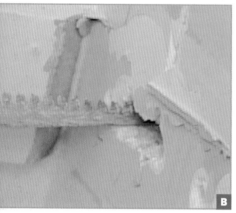

B

◄ MOVING A LIGHT SWITCH TO THE OTHER SIDE OF THE WALL ►

1 Turn off the electricity in the part of the house you're working in. Once you're sure it's off, probe a screwdriver into the wall where you want to put the new switch to feel for an open space. Then trace the outline of a remodel electrical box to mark the area of drywall that needs to be cut out (photo A).

2 Cut the rough opening with a keyhole saw (photo B), also known as a jab saw.

3 Dry-fit the electrical box, then remove the old switch. In this case, the electrical boxes are back to back, so the existing wires could be fed through to the new box (photo C) without any need for wire splicing.

4 Connect the existing wires to a new switch and screw it into place (photo D). Patch the drywall on the other side of the wall.

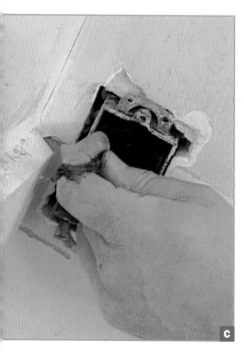

C

D

◢ FINISHING THE SIDES OF STOCK CABINETS ◣

When working with stock or semicustom cabinets, always order extra ¼-inch skins and fill stock to hide little imperfections that come up during the installation. In this case, the homeowners wanted to extend the countertop past the cabinet depth to make a bar seating area. They had to add a support behind the cabinet to hold up this extra counter area, and the side of the support didn't blend with the cabinet (photo A). Here's where the skin comes in handy. Use it to extend the wood finish over the rough area.

A

1 Cut the skin with a table saw to the size that you need. (photo B).

2 Build up the gap on the side of the cabinet with scrap pieces of stock using an impulse nailer (photo C).

3 Use construction adhesive to attach the skin to the side of the cabinet (photo D). Then drive ⅝-inch pin nails to hold the skin in place.

You Will Need

- Safety goggles
- Extra skins
- Scrap stock
- Impulse nailer
- ⅝" pin nails
- Caulking gun
- Construction adhesive
- Table saw with guide

B

C

D

Glossary

back buttering: applying mastic or thinset directly to the back of a tile

back saw: hand saw reinforced with a metal band along its back edge

backsplash: the surface of tile, stone, or metal that protects the wall directly above the kitchen countertop

banquette: a long bench placed against or built into a wall

batten board: scrap piece of lumber used to establish level for setting a first course of wall tiles

beadboard: decorative panels attached vertically on a wall to protect the wall from damage and add architectural style to a room

biscuit: a wafer-sized piece of wood used like a dowel for edge or corner jointing

cement: mixture of limestone and clay powder combined with water to create a solid mass; used in concrete, mortar, or grout; often referred to as portland cement

chalk line: chalk-covered string on a reel that can be pulled taught and snapped to mark straight lines on a surface

concrete: mixture of sand, water, crushed stone, and portland cement

coping saw: handsaw with a thin blade used for cutting small sections out of wood

crown molding: molding installed at the top of a wall at an angle, covering the intersection of wall and ceiling

dovetail joint: a way of making a connection with two pieces of wood using interlocking mortises and tenons; technique used in well-made cabinets and furniture

dowel: a pin inserted into a hole used to fasten two pieces together

drywall: panels of gypsum used to finish walls and ceilings

escutcheon: decorative piece that hides the gap between drywall and a valve sticking out from the wall, or a valve coming out of a countertop

feather: to blend the edges of joint compound with the surrounding wall instead of ending the edges abruptly

field tiles: tiles that fill the center area of a design, as opposed to border or accent tiles

fill stock: extra finished pieces that often come with stock cabinets to fill the gap between the cabinet and the wall

5-in-1 tool: a multiuse hand tool whose flat edge can scrape or spread, pointed edge can clean out small areas, hole in the center can be used as a nail puller, side can open paint cans, and curved edge can squeeze excess paint out of rollers

grout: mixture of water, cement, and sand that can be used to connect materials (like tile) or to create a uniform surface in which to set finish materials

hammer tacker: tool for driving heavy-duty staples into wood surfaces

hole saw: power tool that cuts perfect holes of various sizes in metal, wood, or drywall

impulse nailer: tool that drives nails with the pull of a trigger

jab saw: hand tool for close-quarter cutting that can be used to make plunge cuts and score materials like drywall, plywood, and plastic

Japanese pull saw: hand tool with a flexible, serrated blade; good for getting into tight areas

joint compound: thick, spreadable substance used to fill joints in drywall

joist: steel or wood beams that support floorboards and ceilings

laser level: device that points a level laser line along a wall or floor

level: exactly horizontal

margin float: small version of a grout float that allows you to push grout into tight corners

mastic: adhesive most commonly used to for wall tiles

miter saw: power tool that cuts narrow pieces of wood at an angle; good for cutting trim and molding

molding: wood with a carved profile, as opposed to trim, which is flat

nail set: short piece of metal with a narrow blunt end that is placed on the head of a nail and then hit with a hammer; meant for countersinking nails

pilot hole: a predrilled hole meant to guide a nail or screw

pin nailer: pneumatic nailer that shoots tiny nails; good for attaching light trim pieces

plumb: exactly vertical

plunge cut: to cut directly into the center of an area

pneumatic nailer: an air-powered tool that drives nails of various sizes at the pull of a trigger; has settings to indicate nail depth as well

router: power tool used to make shallow cuts or grooves in wood

shim: a thin piece of wood used to brace or level another piece of wood

skim coat: a thin layer of joint compound or gypsum and spackle applied to a wall to smooth out any rough spots

slake: the process that occurs when mortar is allowed to rest after mixing with water

spline: thin piece of wood that fits into the groove of a piece of tongue-and-groove flooring, allowing you to build out from the groove side by making it into a tongue side

studs: 2 x 4 or 2 x 6 wood beams that make up the interior frame of a wall

subfloor: boards laid over joists to support the finish floor

thinset mortar: a strong mortar designed to adhere well in a thin layer; often used for adhering tile to subfloors

toekick: a recess at the bottom of a cabinet that allows you to

stand next to it without bumping your toes

universal design: the design of products or spaces that can be used with equal success by individuals with or without a disability

wet saw: electric saw whose blade is constantly sprayed with water during cutting to keep it cool; uses a diamond-tipped blade to cut through ceramic as well as stone

Photography Credits

All photographs are courtesy of DIY Network unless otherwise credited.

COURTESY OF AMERICAN STANDARD (www.americanstandard.com): 29 bottom, 45 left

COURTESY OF ARMSTRONG (www.armstrong.com): 31 top, 32 top

COURTESY OF CAESARSTONE QUARTZ SURFACES (877.9QUARTZ, www.caesarstone.com): 36 top

COURTESY OF CORIAN (www.corian.com): 27 top, 34 top

COURTESY OF GREEN MOUNTAIN SOAPSTONE (www.greenmountainsoapstone.com): 35

COURTESY OF KOHLER (www.kohler.com): 16 top, 22, 26 left, 44 top left, 44 bottom left, 44 bottom right, 45 right

COURTESY OF KRAFTMAID CABINETRY (www.kraftmaid.com): 24, 26 right, 28, 29 top, 30, 31 bottom, 33 top, 33 bottom, 38 top, 38 bottom left, 38 bottom right, 39 top right, 39 bottom right

COURTESY OF TOM RALSTON CONCRETE (www.tomralstonconcrete.com): 37 left, 47 bottom

COURTESY OF WILSONART SOLID SURFACE (www.wilsonart.com): 25, 27 bottom, 34 bottom

Metric Conversion Table

Inches	Decimal Inches	Rounded Metric	Inches	Decimal Inches	Rounded Metric	Inches	Decimal Inches	Rounded Metric
1/16	.0625	1.6 mm/.16 cm	7½	7.5	19 cm	18		45.7 cm
1/8	.0125	3 mm/.3 cm	7¾	7.75	19.7 cm	18¼	18.25	46.4 cm
3/16	.1875	5 mm/.5 cm	8		20.3 cm	18½	18.5	47 cm
1/4	.25	6 mm/.6 cm	8¼	8.25	21 cm	18¾	18.75	47.6 cm
5/16	.3125	8 mm/.8 cm	8½	8.5	21.6 cm	19		48.3 cm
3/8	.375	9.5 mm/.95 cm	8¾	8.75	22.2 cm	19¼	19.25	48.9 cm
7/16	.4375	1.1 cm	9		22.9 cm	19½	19.5	49.5 cm
1/2	.5	1.3 cm	9¼	9.25	23.5 cm	19¾	19.75	50.2 cm
9/16	.5625	1.4 cm	9½	9.5	24.1 cm	20		50.8 cm
5/8	.625	1.6 cm	9¾	9.75	24.8 cm	20¼	20.25	51.4 cm
11/16	.6875	1.7 cm	10		25.4 cm	20½	20.5	52.1 cm
3/4	.75	1.9 cm	10¼	10.25	26 cm	20¾	20.75	52.7 cm
13/16	.8125	2.1 cm	10½	10.5	26.7 cm	21		53.3 cm
7/8	.875	2.2 cm	10¾	10.75	27.3 cm	21¼	21.25	54 cm
15/16	.9375	2.4 cm	11		27.9 cm	21½	21.5	54.6 cm
			11¼	11.25	28.6 cm	21¾	21.75	55.2 cm
1		2.5 cm	11½	11.5	29.2 cm	22		55.9 cm
1¼	1.25	3.2 cm	11¾	11.75	30 cm	22¼	22.25	56.5 cm
1½	1.5	3.8 cm	12		30.5 cm	22½	22.5	57.2 cm
1¾	1.75	4.4 cm	12¼	12.25	31.1 cm	22¾	22.75	57.8 cm
2		5 cm	12½	12.5	31.8 cm	23		58.4 cm
2¼	2.25	5.7 cm	12¾	12.75	32.4 cm	23¼	23.25	59 cm
2½	2.5	6.4 cm	13		33 cm	23½	23.5	59.7 cm
2¾	2.75	7 cm	13¼	13.25	33.7 cm	23¾	23.75	60.3 cm
3		7.6 cm	13½	13.5	34.3 cm	24		61 cm
3¼	3.25	8.3 cm	13¾	13.75	35 cm	24¼	24.25	61.6 cm
3½	3.5	8.9 cm	14		35.6 cm	24½	24.5	62.2 cm
3¾	3.75	9.5 cm	14¼	14.25	36.2 cm	24¾	24.75	62.9 cm
4		10.2 cm	14½	14.5	36.8 cm	25		63.5 cm
4¼	4.25	10.8 cm	14¾	14.75	37.5 cm	25¼	25.25	64.1 cm
4½	4.5	11.4 cm	15		38.1 cm	25½	25.5	64.8 cm
4¾	4.75	12 cm	15¼	15.25	38.7 cm	25¾	25.75	65.4 cm
5		12.7 cm	15½	15.5	39.4 cm	26		66 cm
5¼	5.25	13.3 cm	15¾	15.75	40 cm	26¼	26.25	66.7 cm
5½	5.5	14 cm	16		40.6 cm	26½	26.5	67.3 cm
5¾	5.75	14.6 cm	16¼	16.25	41.3 cm	26¾	26.75	68 cm
6		15.2 cm	16½	16.5	41.9 cm	27		68.6 cm
6¼	6.25	15.9 cm	16¾	16.75	42.5 cm	27¼	27.25	69.2 cm
6½	6.5	16.5 cm	17		43.2 cm	27½	27.5	69.9 cm
6¾	6.75	17.1 cm	17¼	17.25	43.8 cm	27¾	27.75	70.5 cm
7		17.8 cm	17½	17.5	44.5 cm	28		71.1 cm
7¼	7.25	18.4 cm	17¾	17.75	45.1 cm			

Index